K

NOT JUST CHINA

Not Just China

The Rise of Recalls in the Age of Global Business

Hari Bapuji

NOT JUST CHINA
Copyright © Hari Bapuji, 2011.

First published in 2011 by
PALGRAVE MACMILLAN®
in the United States—a division of St. Martin's Press LLC,
175 Fifth Avenue, New York, NY 10010.

Where this book is distributed in the UK, Europe and the rest of the world,
this is by Palgrave Macmillan, a division of Macmillan Publishers Limited,
registered in England, company number 785998, of Houndmills,
Basingstoke, Hampshire RG21 6XS.

Palgrave Macmillan is the global academic imprint of the above companies
and has companies and representatives throughout the world.

Palgrave® and Macmillan® are registered trademarks in the United States,
the United Kingdom, Europe and other countries.

ISBN: 978–0–230–10451–8

Library of Congress Cataloging-in-Publication Data

Bapuji, Hari.
    Not just China : the rise of recalls in the age of global business / Hari
Bapuji.
        p. cm.
    Includes bibliographical references and index.
    ISBN 978–0–230–10451–8 (hardback)
        1. Product recall—United States. 2. Product safety—United States.
    3. Products liability—United States. I. Title.

HF5415.9.B37 2010
363.19—dc22   2010024469

A catalogue record of the book is available from the British Library.

Design by Newgen Imaging Systems (P) Ltd., Chennai, India.

First edition: January 2011

D 10 9 8 7 6 5 4 3

Printed in the United States of America.

To

All of you, who helped me to conduct and communicate this research

Contents

Figures and Tables

Figures

Tables

Preface

I was drawn to research recalls almost by coincidence. It is not often that a researcher can point to a particular date when his or her research on a particular topic began. However, I can clearly point to August 14, 2007 as the day when my research into product recalls began. On that day, Mattel recalled millions of toys made in China and cited supplier failures as the reason behind recalls. The story was all over the media, with analysts asking for increased surveillance and recommending the boycott of Chinese products. There were also questions as to whether China could survive the impending backlash. I was quite surprised by the passionate arguments and decided to study the recalls closely. Soon, I realized that the debate surrounding the recalls was full of misconceptions and misinformation. Obviously, it was at least partly a result of lack of research on the topic.

Since then, I have researched recalls, particularly toy recalls. In the course of my research, I have found that the communications by companies during a recall rarely spell out the exact reasons for recall. By their very nature, recalls are negative events and it is perhaps understandable that managers do not want too much information to get out. But, in the absence of clear information, in-depth studies that generate proper understanding are not possible. As a result, misconceptions abound; consumers feel outraged, but do not know what to do.

The recalls in 2007 have catapulted consumer safety into the center of public consciousness, but its place was sustained by the continuing recalls of peanut butter, cars, drugs, and a number of other products in the years that followed. Despite the increased awareness, the debate on recalls and product safety, in general, is riddled with anecdotes and emotional reactions rather than objective study of the underlying causes of recalls and ways to prevent future recalls.

This book aims to inform the debate on consumer safety by using data on U.S. toy recalls over the last two decades to examine some common misconceptions as well as unearth hitherto unexplored issues. The analysis in this book shows that country of origin is essentially a red herring. In order to improve consumer product safety, we need to understand the *reasons for recalls*, such as imperfect designs and inadequate organizational systems. Further, we must examine the *responsiveness of recalling companies* as reflected in the time they took to recall, the amount of harm that occurred before they issued recalls, and the efforts companies make to recover the recalled products. Finally, it is important to study *reactions of consumers* and other stakeholders to counter any possible misconceptions. Focusing resources on the wrong areas may run counter to the goal of improved consumer safety.

This book does not claim to be an authoritative pronouncement on recalls. Instead, in the tradition of true science, it only aims to bring data to the fore to dispel some faulty assumptions. In other words, the purpose of this book is not to establish the truth, but to alleviate misconceptions that have dogged the recall debate in general. I hope that the ensuing debate, devoid of misinformation and falsities, can help all the stakeholders to focus on improving consumer product safety in a comprehensive manner rather than attend only to issues that are popular but might not reflect the major challenges to consumer safety.

*   *   *

Every scientific work is a collaborative venture in which ideas from several known and unknown sources are integrated to develop a cogent picture. In addition, several stakeholders support the research directly or indirectly by encouraging the effort. I did not find any dearth of supporters, collaborators, and critics. It is difficult to name them all here, but I would like to acknowledge the help of several people who have been behind me in this research.

When I look back, my research on recalls took the direction it did because of a chance discussion I had with Dean Feltham, who immediately saw the potential of this research and encouraged me to go after it full steam. As I pursued this research, Paul Beamish enthusiastically collaborated with me, although this area was new to him and the publications arising from it were not traditional scholarly publications. Since then, I collaborated with Sergio Carvalho, Mary Crossan, Niraj Dawar, Manpreet Hora, Andre Laplume, E. Muralidharan, and Kent Walker to examine several issues related to recalls—I learned much from all of them. In addition, a number of my friends and well-wishers constantly encouraged me to pursue this research by reading everything that I wrote and offering their valuable comments. These include Chetan Joshi, Balaji Koka, Sudha Mani, Raza Mir, Srinivas Sridharan, and Suhaib Riaz, whose support I could never be thankful enough for.

In conducting this research and communicating it, I have received enormous support from the University of Manitoba and people there. Tamara Bodi worked tirelessly to coordinate with the media and communicate my research to them in very creative ways. I received able research assistance from Bhanu Duggirala, Umesh Gungiah, and Kevin Morris, besides many others. Several colleagues, including Parshotam Dass, Subbu Sivaramakrishnan, Nick Turner, Judy Wilson, and Xioayun Wang proved to be my source of sustenance on a daily basis.

In addition to above, I received great support from many people around the world, covering the entire spectrum of product safety stakeholders. These people, who had never met me before, have generously offered their time and insights. Unfortunately, I am not allowed to name many (perhaps any) of them. However, I would like to acknowledge the constant support of Marla Felcher, who helped enormously, purely because she believed in the importance of research on this topic.

My research on recalls has been supported by two generous grants from the Social Sciences and Humanities Research Council of Canada and a number of small grants from the University of Manitoba. As I wrote this book, Michele Ebel was a great help; she copy edited the manuscript several times in a very prompt and efficient manner. Laurie Harting and her team at Palgrave Macmillan were quite supportive as I wrote the manuscript.

Finally, I have no words to express appreciation for my wife, Sunita, and son, Siddharth. They endured my erratic work habits and accommodated my idiosyncrasies. Without their understanding, I would never have been able to write this book.

Thank you all! I greatly appreciate your support!

Hari Bapuji

Prologue

Barking up the Wrong Tree

On November 26, 2009, a CBC News producer from Toronto contacted me to ask some questions about the Chinese-made parts that had been the subject of a massive crib recall only a few days before. She was referring to the crib recall announced on November 23, 2009, by the U.S. Consumer Product Safety Commission (CPSC) and Health Canada, in cooperation with Stork Craft Manufacturing.[1] This recall involved a Canadian company, affected more than 2.1 million drop-side cribs, and concerned millions of parents in both the United States and Canada. As Canada's national broadcaster, CBC News wanted to do a story that would inform and educate parents about the issue.

The reporter began our conversation with a very blunt question: Was the recall due to poor manufacturing by Stork Craft's Chinese suppliers? I pointed out that since the recall involved cribs that had been made in Canada, China, and Indonesia, it was reasonable to conclude that the problem was not necessarily due solely to manufacturing issues in China. Further, Stork Craft had made and sold the subject cribs for nearly 17 years, between January 1993 and October 2009, and since China had become a manufacturing hub in only the last decade or so, its manufacturing practices were not likely the root of the problem.

The reporter then asked me whether the recall was due to poor manufacturing in general, since the problems with the recalled cribs included plastic hardware that could break or deform, or from which parts were missing. I highlighted the fact that only those cribs with plastic hardware had been recalled and not those with metal drop-side hardware. At some point in the evolution of crib-making, Stork Craft, and possibly other crib manufacturers as well, had decided to use plastic instead of metal hardware, perhaps due to costs or other considerations. In fact, the recall pertained only to drop-side cribs, not to rigid-side cribs, and the repair for the recalled cribs essentially involved turning the drop-side crib into a rigid-side crib. Further, regulators and industry associations had begun to advise against making and selling drop-side cribs. In other words, over a period of time, it had become clear that the drop-side feature had inherent problems in its design. Hence, the recall likely had nothing to do with how the cribs were manufactured, but rather with how they were designed.

I explained that another problem with the drop-side cribs was that parents could inadvertently install them upside down, which compromised the integrity of the product. As a result, the drop-sides could become detached, entrapping children or causing them to fall. In a similar situation, for example, Aqua-Leisure recalled inflatable pool ladders because some had been installed incorrectly by users, which caused the ladders to break and injure the users.[2] As part of its recall, Aqua-Leisure provided new assembly instructions and color-coded support clips, all of which reduced, if not eliminated, the chance of incorrect assembly. In other words, in order to be very safe, a product design must take into account use and abuse, as well as the potential for incorrect assembly.

Our discussion then turned to other issues related to the crib recall, in particular to the fact that it had taken such a long time for the problem to be realized and for a recall to be announced. The recall had been announced only after 110 incidents, which included four suffocations, 20 falls and 15 entrapments. Knowing, even in hindsight, that some of these injuries and deaths could have been prevented through a different design or through the use of metal hardware can be a difficult burden to bear, certainly for parents, but also for companies. As the recall notices do not provide information related to when these incidents occurred or to how fast the company acted, it is difficult to tell whether Stork Craft acted swiftly enough to eliminate the hazard as soon as its potential for harm was recognized.

As our conversation concluded, my interviewer asked whether I felt that focusing on China in this case was akin to barking up the wrong tree. I replied that Chinese manufacturing was not without its problems, but recalls should be examined very closely in order to clearly understand what factors had actually caused them instead of automatically blaming manufacturing or China, for that matter. Given the evolution of global supply chains in the recent past, manufacturing companies have been able to spread their designing, sourcing, and assembling activities across the globe. As a result, it has become increasingly difficult to pinpoint the source of a problem and ensure product safety.

* * *

My conversation with the CBC reporter reminded me of my first-ever interview with CBC Radio in Winnipeg, on August 14, 2007, the day Mattel announced a large recall of toys. Since that time, my research has revolved around product recalls and has taken off in several directions. Although consumer product safety is an important issue, up to this point, very little research and public discussion has focused on the intricacies of recalls and the various dimensions that need to be examined. Hence, this book is an effort to cast light on some of those dimensions by analyzing the toy recalls announced in the United States since 1990. I hope that the contents of this book will spur more research on product recalls and generate a nuanced debate on consumer product safety.

The book is organized as follows. Chapter 1 sets the context by describing the sudden rise in product recalls in 2007, with an in-depth discussion of a few high-profile recalls such as those of toothpaste, pet foods, tires, and toys. Each of these recalls occurred for a different reason, but all were due to missteps at different parts of the global supply chain. These discussions and examples underscore the global nature of the production of today's consumer products. Then, the effect of recalls on consumer confidence is discussed, along with the implications of recalls for global trade. Considering that products are rarely made within the boundaries of a single company or within the borders of a single country, this chapter highlights the need to examine the issue of product recalls thoroughly.

Chapter 2 presents the regulatory framework that deals with consumer product safety and outlines the growth in recalls over the years. Most current studies that examine recalls have focused on the recall announcements. This method does not, however, provide a complete picture, since a recall notice for 20 units and one for 2 million units are both counted in the same manner. Therefore, chapter 2 discusses the growth in recalls in terms of the number of recall announcements and the number of toys recalled each year. The analysis in this chapter shows that while recalls have increased dramatically, the number of units recalled has not witnessed a similar increase. This chapter speculates about a number of possible reasons for the growth in recalls, all of which the subsequent chapters examine empirically.

Chapter 3 presents a history of toy imports over the years and of the growth in Chinese imports. During the last four decades, toy manufacturing has shifted away from the Western countries, first to Japan, then to Hong Kong and Taiwan, and then to China. Over the last decade, and particularly since China's entry into the World Trade Organization (WTO), toy imports from China have increased at a rapid pace. Simultaneously, recalls of toys made in China have also increased. This chapter compares the share of Chinese-made toys in recalls with the share of Chinese products in U.S. toy imports to show that while the share of Chinese-made toy recalls remains lower than China's imports share, the former has been increasing in the recent years.

Chapter 4 tests a very common assumption about recalled products: that recalls affect lower-priced products more than they affect higher-priced products. The analysis, however, shows that recalls of higher-priced products have been traditionally lower, but have been increasing over the recent past and now account for more recalls. This trend is true for toys made in China and elsewhere. In fact, the recalls of lower-priced products made in other countries (other than China) have seen an increase in the last five years. The analysis in this chapter questions the common assumption that cost pressures on Chinese manufacturers have resulted in recalls, particularly of lower-priced products.

Chapter 5 presents a discussion on the global toy industry to suggest that while toys are made in China, they are often designed in the non-Asian headquarters of toy companies. This chapter draws on the CPSC investigations and judicial pronouncements in order to illustrate the difference between design flaws and manufacturing flaws. Simply put, a design flaw refers to the manner in which a product is visualized. In contrast to a manufacturing flaw, which arises due to materials used and actual manufacturing practices, a design flaw will result in a defective product from the start, irrespective of where the product is made. This chapter analyzes toy recalls for design and manufacturing flaws and points out that a vast majority of toy recalls, both those made in China and elsewhere, were necessitated by inadequate designs rather than improper manufacturing.

Building on the discussion of the global toy industry in the previous chapter, chapter 6 examines the disconnect between design and manufacturing in global toy supply chains. This disconnect has enabled the active and direct participation of retailers and distributors in the value chain. In contrast to the toy companies, the retailers and distributors do not specialize in toys and thus have limited knowledge about any potential problems when they select a particular toy for commerce. Not surprisingly, the recalls by this group have increased notably in the recent past. More importantly, the analysis in this chapter shows that retailers and distributors have been less responsive than manufacturers in addressing product safety issues.

Chapter 7 delves further into company responsiveness and examines the speed with which recalls have been announced. Consumers are apt to return the recalled products if the products are recalled swiftly, that is, before consumers get used to using them. Once consumers are accustomed to using the product, they might ignore the recall warnings. Therefore, it is important to issue recalls promptly. However, the analysis in this chapter shows that companies have recently slowed their overall recall process, and thus there is an increase in the time to recall. This chapter also discusses how lead-tainted toys that had been sold in the market for years were recalled in 2007, leading to a sudden spurt in recalls in that year.

Building on the need for swift recalls, chapter 8 discusses the need to also issue a recall in a preventive fashion—before incidents and injuries occur. The analysis, however, shows that companies are issuing more recalls in a reactive fashion recently, only after the defective products have caused harm. This chapter also discusses how companies sometimes fail to report incidents and injuries associated with their products, thus causing delay and increasing harm to consumers. As a result of such non-responsiveness by companies, the fines levied by the CPSC have also been increasing in recent years.

An important component of a recall is the remedy offered to the consumers (in the form of refund, replacement, repair, or instruction to discard) for the recalled products. The remedy offered influences the number of products that consumers actually return. Chapter 9 examines how the remedy offered by companies has decreased in the recent years from refund to replacement or even to replacement with a toy of lesser value. As a result of this tendency toward a lesser remedy, consumers are unlikely to return the dangerous products. Consequently, even when a recall is issued, the danger may not be reduced as a large number of products remain in the hands of consumers.

Integrating the analysis from the previous chapters, chapter 10 presents the steps managers can take to prevent recalls. These steps relate to developing sound designs, ensuring manufacturing integrity, and communicating the correct assembly and use of products to consumers. Chapter 11 complements this discussion, presenting the various stakeholders in toy safety and examining their role and influence in ensuring product safety. In particular, this chapter discusses the role of regulators and consumers in enhancing consumer product safety. Further, this chapter draws upon extant research on product recalls to present a future research agenda that will provide a well-rounded perspective on product recalls.

Finally, the epilogue deals with the large recall of automobiles by Toyota in 2010, discussing it within the context of the book's findings and in terms of the broader lessons that should be drawn from the recalls of non-consumer products. The epilogue concludes with a brief discussion of recalls by Johnson & Johnson and McDonald's to point out that focusing on country of manufacture does not necessarily improve product safety. Instead, the discussion should be directed at understanding the organizational systems and processes that contribute to recalls and their effective management. More specifically, the focus should be on reasons for recalls, responsiveness of companies, and reactions of consumers.

Chapter 1

2007: The Year of the Recall

Product recalls are not new or uncommon, but, in an unprecedented way, the year 2007 brought recalls to the top of the agenda for businesses, regulators, consumers, and governments. From the start of the year, manufacturers recalled several products made in China. While it is unfair to say that Chinese manufacturing practices have been mostly responsible for the recent growth in recalls, it is not inaccurate to say that they have made a significant contribution to the spike. Certainly, we can cite several examples of unsafe behaviors during the subject timeframe. Included in this list are products such as pet food, tires, toys, and counterfeit toothpaste. Each one of these categories has a different story, but in nearly every case, the recalls occurred following investigations by unsuspecting customers who examined the products and reported an issue to the authorities. In some sense, the seeds of the 2007 recall wave took root in Panama.

The Panamanian Tremor that Shook China and the World

In 2006, Panamanian health authorities bought 46 barrels of pharmaceutical-grade glycerine syrup from a Panamanian broker called Medicom Business Group. The syrup was identified as 99.5 percent pure glycerine and was sold to Medicom by Spain-based Rasfer International. Rasfer had purchased the syrup from a Beijing-based trading company called CNSC Fortune Way, which was a unit of a Chinese government-owned business. The syrup was originally made by a Chinese factory, Taixing Glycerine Factory, which was not in fact authorized to sell medical ingredients. It is believed that Taixing bought the glycerine from some other supplier in China, but since it is common for agents not to list the names of their suppliers so that buyers do not bypass them (the agents) in future transactions, it was difficult to trace the source.

As the syrup traveled from one company to another within a global supply chain that involved China, Spain, and Panama, no one tested to see whether the syrup was actually 99.5 percent glycerine, as the seller had asserted. In reality, the syrup was contaminated by diethylene glycol, a substance that looks and acts like glycerine but is much cheaper than the real thing. Unknowingly, the authorities in Panama mixed the imported syrup into 260,000 bottles of cold medicine and then distributed them to the general population.[1]

The patients who consumed the cold medicine were poisoned, many fatally. Unfortunately, the deadly cough syrup was the least likely suspect in these deaths, and authorities looked into a number of other possible causes for the poisonings. It took a Herculean effort by the Panamanian health authorities to trace the source of the poisonings and deaths. When the source of the poison was finally identified, Panamanian authorities conducted a nationwide campaign informing people to stop using the cough syrup and discard the bottles.[2]

On May 5, 2007, a Panamanian consumer, Eduardo Arias, read the label on a 59-cent tube of toothpaste and realized that it contained diethylene glycol. Because of the recent poisonings in Panama and the resulting public awareness, it quickly dawned on Arias that the toothpaste contained the very same substance that had already killed dozens of his fellow Panamanians. Arias bought a tube of the toothpaste and turned it over to authorities. The tube did not list where the toothpaste was made, but the source was later traced to China. When the authorities in Panama announced their findings, alarm bells were set off around the world.

Within a few weeks, it became clear that the counterfeit toothpaste had been sold not only in Panama but in several countries across the globe. As a result, officials in over 30 countries—including the United States, Canada, Spain, France, Europe, Mexico, Kenya, Vietnam, Japan, Britain, Australia, and New Zealand—recalled millions of toothpaste tubes. Several popular brands of toothpaste were affected by the recall, including Colgate, Mr. Cool, Excel, Dentamint, and Sensodyne.

As millions of toothpaste tubes were recalled, it dawned upon consumers that all was not well with imported products. Soon, the risk extended into areas besides toothpaste. For example, in the same year, the pet food industry took a huge hit.

Recalls that Shocked the Pet World

In February 2007, a Canadian pet food company called Menu Foods received complaints from consumers who stated that their cats and dogs that had eaten Menu Foods' products were developing kidney failure. Menu Foods conducted a battery of tests revealing that the problem may have stemmed from a supply of wheat gluten that the company had sourced from a Las Vegas supplier called ChemNutra. ChemNutra had purchased the wheat gluten from Xuozhou Anying, a Chinese company. However, in order to avoid inspections and taxes, the product had been imported through a textiles company called Suzhou Textiles.

Unfortunately, a problem at Menu Foods was bound to affect the entire pet food industry because the company supplied pet foods that were sold under private labels by many leading companies, including Nestlé, Procter & Gamble, Mars, Colgate, and Del Monte. It was estimated that the products of Menu Foods accounted for nearly 40 percent of all pet foods sold in the United States and 75 percent of those sold in Canada, under various brands. Not surprisingly, all these companies issued recalls.

In the following weeks, as reports of pet illness and death mounted, a number of companies, research laboratories, and the U.S. Food and Drug Administration (FDA) became involved in order to find the source of the problem in the wheat gluten. In late March 2007, it became evident that the wheat gluten sourced by ChemNutra from China had been contaminated with melamine. Additional probing identified a second material—a rice protein concentrate used in pet foods—that was also contaminated with melamine. Investigations revealed that all the contaminated material came from two Chinese factories, Xuozhou Anying and Binzhou Futian.

As the toll mounted and the number of recalls increased, it became evident that the melamine had been added deliberately to the pet food in order to increase protein counts during the testing process. Instead of adding soy, wheat, or corn protein, the suppliers had added melamine, which mimicked protein in tests *and* was five times cheaper. The practice of adding melamine to animal feed was an open secret among those in the business in China, but it was not known to those on the outside.[3] The large-scale use of melamine in animal feed was not only a danger to pets, but also to hogs, chickens, and fish produced for human consumption. Although melamine in small quantities was not known to affect humans, neither was it a desirable ingredient to ingest.

The degree of penetration of the contaminated animal feed within the U.S. food supply chain resulted in a huge casualty rate: over 14,000 cases of illness, including over 4,000 deaths of cats and dogs. Further, the contamination resulted in a wave of pet food recalls involving over 60 million units of product by 18 companies, 200 brands, and 5,300 product lines.[4] Reports from around the world began to put pressure on the Chinese government, which initially resisted investigations. However, as the pressure mounted, the government began to crack down on offenders. Several officials of the state food and drug administration were arrested and prosecuted. In an extreme step, the country's chief food and drug regulator was executed, an act that did more to confirm the widespread corruption in China than it did to allay the concerns of global consumers, especially when the recalls began to expand from the food and drug arena into other areas such as tires and toys.

A Gum Strip that Became a Sticking Point

As a small company in Union, New Jersey, Foreign Tire Sales (FTS) was set up in 1973 when its founder began importing tires from Korea while he was still a student. Since that time, FTS has imported tires from Korea, Thailand, the former Yugoslavia, and China. According to FTS, the company now owns over four hundred tire molds from which over 150 different types of tires are produced. Despite the scope of its operations, FTS has a staff of only seven people.[5]

Since 1990, FTS has bought and imported tires from Hangzhou Zongce (HZ), China's second-largest tire maker. Eventually, FTS contracted HZ to manufacture radial tires for vans, SUVs, and light trucks. These tires had been imported into the United States since 2002 and were sold under brand names such as Westlake, Compass, and YKS. As stipulated in the contract, the tires were required to include a gum strip between the steel bands in order to prevent the tire treads from separating. Since the Firestone recall of millions of tires in 2000, after hundreds of deaths and injuries, tread separation had become a significant concern in the United States.

It may be noted that although FTS was a tire importer, as is typical of most importers, the company did not physically handle the tires it brought into the country. In other words, FTS never saw the products it imported; contract manufacturers such as HZ shipped the tires directly to FTS customers.

About three years into the new contract, in October 2005, FTS noticed a sharp increase in customer complaints about the

HZ-manufactured radial tires. The company decided to investigate the matter. According to FTS, HZ had unilaterally omitted the gum strips or had used gum strips that were not large enough. In fact, FTS claimed that HZ officials had actually admitted to this practice in September 2006.

In June 2007, FTS informed the National Highway Traffic Safety Administration (NHTSA) about the problems with HZ's tires and asked for help to issue a recall of 450,000 tires. Not surprisingly, NHTSA was displeased with FTS, who had taken nearly two years to inform NHTSA about the danger of the tires. It was alleged that FTS reported the problem to NHTSA only after the company itself had been named as a defendant in a lawsuit over an accident in which two persons had been killed and another severely injured.[6]

HZ's version of the story, however, was quite different. The company denied any wrongdoing and argued that the allegations that it omitted gum strips were an effort to undercut the growing influence of Chinese manufacturers in the global tire market and particularly in the U.S. market.[7] Perhaps there was a modicum of truth in HZ's statements: tire imports to the United States from China had tripled in a span of four years and were estimated to have led to a loss of five thousand jobs in the United States.[8] Even so, it was widely believed that the omission of the gum strip was only a reflection of a larger problem plaguing Chinese manufacturing: the issue of factories cutting corners after winning a contract. A couple of high-profile toy recalls brought this problem further into focus.

Toy Recalls: Far from Child's Play

The toy company RC2 owes its success to its license deals with Disney, Nickelodeon, Sesame Street, Thomas & Friends, and Winnie the Pooh, all of which gave RC2 an exclusive right to produce and sell their toys. Like many toy companies in the United States, RC2 outsourced its production to factories in China and did not own any manufacturing facilities. It did, however, employ 175 people in China to coordinate with its network of contract manufacturers.

On March 29, 2007, RC2 was notified by one of its U.S. retail customers that the surface paint on a Thomas & Friends toy contained lead in excess of permissible limits of 0.06 percent.[9] This toy was produced at one of RC2's dedicated contract manufacturers, Overseas Winner Limited (OWL). Upon learning this information, RC2 promptly began investigations to identify the extent of the problem and concluded that the toys made by OWL (but not by other contractors) between January 2005 and April 2007 did in fact have excess lead in their surface paint. Accordingly, RC2 contacted the CPSC and, on June 13, 2007, recalled a total of 1.5 million toys that had been sold from January 2005 through June 2007.

Continued testing by RC2 revealed that 200,000 additional toys produced by OWL and by another dedicated contract manufacturer, 3i Corporation, also contained excess lead in their surface paint. Following this discovery, RC2 issued another recall on September 26, 2007 that included the 200,000 additional toys. Later in 2007, this recall was followed by two additional recalls for the same problem. In other words, RC2 issued four separate recalls in 2007, involving a total of 1.86 million toys.

RC2 faced serious difficulties in handling the recall. First, it offered to provide a replacement toy to the consumers but asked them to pay for the postage. The company relented in response to the ensuing consumer outrage and offered to reimburse postage to those who asked for it. Second, in an effort to placate the owners of the recalled toys, RC2 included a gift along with the replacement toys. Unfortunately, one of the gift toys (Toad Vehicle) also contained excess lead and was later recalled. Third, the company was unavailable to media and consumers for days after the recall and began to communicate only after its silence had backfired.

Curt Stoelting, CEO of RC2, gave his first media interview five weeks after the recall, explaining that his company was using the recall to improve procedures and safeguards. He asserted that RC2 had always required its suppliers to follow company safety specifications, but in the case of the incident that had caused the recall, those requirements had not been met. Mattel not only adopted this line of defense but took it to a new height when it issued its own recall soon after.

As the industry leader, with annual sales of over $5 billion, Mattel pioneered many trends that defined the course of the toy industry, including the offshoring of toy production. Although it owned some factories in China, Mattel also operated through a large network of contract manufacturers in order to produce its toys.

In June 2007, Auchan, a French-owned direct importer of Mattel's products, performed pre-shipment tests with the help of an independent laboratory called Intertek. These tests revealed that Mattel's toys, made by a vendor called Lee Der Industrial Company, contained lead levels that were above permissible limits. In a related incident, a consumer in the United States informed Mattel on June 27, 2007 that a home test kit had identified excessive lead in a Mattel toy. Following these reports, Mattel ramped up its testing and investigation, focusing particularly on Lee Der, since that company manufactured both toys.

Lee Der Industrial Company was located in Foshan City of Guangdong Province, the home of thousands of small toy factories. Mattel had initially hired Lee Der to make a small batch of educational toys in 1993. By July 2007, Lee Der employed approximately 2,500 people and made toys almost exclusively for Mattel. Lee Der had been purchasing its paint from Dongxing New Energy Company since 2003. The owner of Dongxing was a good friend of Lee Der's co-owner, Cheung Shu-hung. When Dongxing ran out of yellow pigment in April 2007, it sourced about 330 pounds of it from Dongguan Zhongxin Toner Powder Factory, and in turn supplied the paint to Lee Der, who then used it on Mattel's toys. Initial reports suggested that the owners of the Dongguan Zhongxin Toner Powder Factory were not traceable and that the company was a fake.

Following its internal investigations, Mattel contacted the Consumer Product Safety Commission (CPSC) and recalled 967,000 units of nearly 50 different toys sold between May 2007 and August 2007. While this recall was underway, even more instances of excess lead in surface paint came to light, this time on Sarge cars. These toys were made for Mattel by Early Light Industrial Company, Ltd. of Hong Kong, produced in its manufacturing facility located in Pinghu, China.[10] Early Light had supplied toys to Mattel for 20 years. Mattel again contacted the CPSC and recalled 253,000 Sarge cars sold between May 2007 and August 2007.

In addition to the toys recalled for excess lead, Mattel also expanded one of its previous recalls of Polly Pocket sets sold between May 2003 and September 2006. These sets, also made in China, were recalled because the magnets in the toys were coming loose and were then being swallowed by children. When more than one was swallowed, these powerful magnets tried to "find each other" inside children's stomachs, causing intestinal ruptures. In an expansion of the magnet-related recall, Mattel announced that it was recalling nearly ten million toys, including play sets like Polly Pocket, Doggie Day Care, Barbie, and Tanner, as well as action figures such as Batman and One Piece.

In announcing the recalls for excess lead and loose magnets, Robert Eckert, Mattel's CEO stated, "The Cars toy was produced by Early Light Industrial Company, one of Mattel's contract manufacturing facilities in China, which subcontracted the painting of parts of the toy to another vendor named Hong Li Da, also in China. While the painting subcontractor was required to utilize certified paint supplied directly from Early Light, he had instead violated Mattel standards and utilized paint from a non-authorized third-party supplier. To address this issue we have immediately implemented a strengthened three-point check system." In other words, taking the RC2 line further, Mattel asserted that the recalls occurred because its contract manufacturers failed to follow Mattel's standards, stating that "We were failed, and so we failed you."

In the weeks that followed, Mattel issued five more recalls for excess lead in the surface paint of toys. Several other companies quickly followed suit by issuing recalls of Chinese-made goods. About 40 different products, most made in China, were recalled for excess lead. As the widespread recalls were announced, parents went about the task of emptying their household's toy baskets, which, for obvious reasons, was upsetting to their children. Some families filed class-action lawsuits, asking Mattel to pay for tests to determine whether the children had been exposed to lead.

The Aftermath of the Recalls

Coming on top of several earlier recalls related to toothpaste, tires, and pet food, the news of Mattel's recalls spread like wildfire all over the world. The media coverage of the toy recalls was unprecedented, with TV channels running the story throughout the day on August 14, 2007. One of the greatest casualties of this spate of recalls was consumer confidence. In a poll conducted by Reuters/Zogby,[11] the majority of people (close to 80 percent) reported that they were apprehensive about buying goods made in China. Nearly two-thirds (63 percent) of the respondents reported that they were likely to participate in a boycott of Chinese-made goods until the Chinese government improved its regulations governing the safety of the goods exported to the United States. Several other opinion polls conducted by news agencies and market research firms revealed similar sentiments. Analysts pointed their fingers at the many previous recalls of Chinese-made goods and demanded government action from both the United States and China.

The governments in the West were quick to respond to this crisis of confidence. At a Canadian summit of North American political leaders, the heads of the governments of Canada, the United States, and Mexico decided to crack down on unsafe goods, particularly those designed for children. In the European Union, Consumer Commissioner Meglena Kuneva initiated a broad review of the strengths and weaknesses of the consumer product safety mechanisms in Europe. This review involved extensive work with national sur-veillance authorities, the Chinese authorities, the U.S. authorities, and the European toy industry and retailers, as well as consultations with the European Parliament. In Brazil, the government decided to halt the import of Mattel toys until the lead issue was resolved.

The U.S. Senate and Congress held hearings on the safety of imported products, and Mattel's CEO, Bob Eckert, was summoned to testify in both the hearings. In those hearings, Eckert asserted that "a few vendors, either deliberately or out of carelessness, circum-vented our long-established safety standards and procedures."

The recalls catapulted consumer product safety to the center of a heated debate. Questions were raised about whether the CPSC had enough resources to ensure product safety. Consumer advocates and some politicians pointed to the steady budget and staffing cuts the CPSC faced; with 420 employees in 2007, the CPSC was half the size it had been in the 1980s. Many wondered whether that number was adequate to monitor 15,000 consumer products in a market valued at $614 billion. It was pointed out that CPSC had only one employee devoted to testing the safety of toys. Also, only 15 CPSC inspectors were available to check all the U.S. ports where import shipments were received.[12]

In addition to not having enough resources, the CPSC also had limited powers. For example, it could only impose a maximum pen-alty of $1.8 million on erring companies. Moreover, imposing any penalties at all was quite difficult because the burden of proof rested with the CPSC. In addition, according to legal requirements, the CPSC could not even make public its concerns about or investigations of particular companies and products until it had gained the approval of the companies whose names were being divulged.[13]

This ongoing attention to the issue of recalls began to affect the image of all toys made outside the United States. Understandably, consumers began to scrutinize every toy to find out where it was manufactured before they made a purchase. Many consumers rushed out in search of toys made in the United States or in other developed countries, but these turned out to be hard to find. Undeterred, some enthusiasts set up Web sites to inform shoppers about where to buy American toys (e.g., www.howtobuyamerican.com), and others set up businesses that sold only those toys that were *not* made in China, including the aptly named NMC Toys (Not Made in China Toys, www.nmctoys.com). A few companies, such as Little Tykes, which already manufactured some of their toys in the United States, began to prominently display "Made in USA" labels on their products.

Some analysts argued that the suppliers in China and elsewhere were compromising on safety to meet the ever-increasing pressure of Western companies to supply toys and other products at a cheaper cost, even in the face of increasing raw material demands and wage costs—a double-squeeze for the toy suppliers. Some consumer advocates asserted that, no matter where in the global supply chain the problem might have occurred, companies (like Mattel) that brought toys into the United States had the primary responsibility for ensuring the safety of those products.

The effect of the recalls could also be seen in the already-besieged toy suppliers in China. Cheung Shu-hung, who directly managed the operations of Lee Der, committed suicide on August 11, 2007. Following the recalls, many Chinese employees at Lee Der and other factories lost their jobs; for those who did remain, workplace conditions became an issue of discussion. How had the lead affected the employees who had painted it onto the toys, and thus were exposed to it, every day of the week?

The recalls began to severely erode "Brand China." In an attempt to stem the tide of the fallout, the Chinese government quickly set up a taskforce under the leadership of Chinese Vice Premier Wu Yi to improve and ensure product safety. This taskforce intensified inspections of Chinese plants and suspended or revoked the export licenses of hundreds of companies. Some of the suppliers who had been named in the recalls were jailed. Faced with intense pressure from all quarters, the Chinese authorities asserted that the majority of products made in China were safe and that Western companies were unduly blaming China. Several suppliers who worked with big companies and who had been forced to close factories or lay off workers asserted that large companies in the West were using them as scapegoats.[14]

In what appeared to be a counteroffensive, China rejected some North American imports, including frozen pig kidneys from the United States and frozen pork spareribs from Canada. These products were found to contain residues of ractopamine, a substance that was forbidden for use as a veterinary medicine in China. China also rejected shipments of U.S.-made orange pulp and dried apricots that contained high levels of bacteria and preservatives.[15]

*   *   *

The number and variety of recalls of made-in-China products in 2007 have catapulted the issue of consumer product safety onto the world stage. The recall issue has managed to shake consumer confidence, spur lawmakers into action, galvanize consumer advocates, and open a new dialogue on the safety of imported products. However, the solution is more complex than simply increasing the surveillance of imported products. Even though a given item might be assembled in and marked as originating in a particular country, in today's world, the final product is rarely the result of efforts within the borders of a single country or even within the boundaries of a single company. As global supply chains span the world in a relentless race to cut costs and reduce effort, nearly all modern-day products are hybrids in which design, engineering, sourcing of components, manufacturing, testing, and distribution occur in different parts of the world. Even simple products like T-shirts and jeans are no longer made only in one country.[16]

Some analysts argue that global supply chains have increased operational and quality risks for companies. As a result, it is not surprising that products made in China are recalled more often in today's commercial climate. Others point to the lack of research on recalls and suggest that a few high-profile recalls are not evidence of systematic problems with China and other emerging economies.[17] Therefore, there is a pressing need to closely examine the phenomenon of recalls in order to understand the reasons behind them and their apparent growth and, more importantly, to ensure consumer product safety. Toward this end, the next chapter asks the question: Have recalls really increased in the recent years in a systematic manner?

Chapter 2

Toy Recalls: Up, Up, and Up

A number of federal agencies manage the safety of consumer goods in the United States. Three of them are responsible for most of the products a typical consumer uses. The Food and Drug Administration (FDA) has jurisdiction over foods, drugs, and cosmetics. The National Highway Traffic Safety Administration (NHTSA) oversees the safety of cars, trucks, motorcycles, and these vehicles' accessories, such as tires and car seats. The Consumer Product Safety Commission (CPSC) has jurisdiction over any product that is used in a residence or school, or for recreational or personal use.

Other agencies handle products that fall outside the jurisdiction of the CPSC, FDA, and NHTSA. For example, the Environmental Protection Agency (EPA) oversees pesticides, rodenticides, and fungicides.The Bureau of Alcohol, Tobacco, Firearms, and Explosives (ATF) monitors the products that make up its name. The U.S. Coast Guard handles boats and other watercraft, including personal flotation devices. The U.S. Chemical Safety and Hazard Investigation Board manages the safety of chemicals.

Consumer Product Safety Commission

The CPSC is an independent U.S. federal regulatory agency that Congress created in response to the 1972 Consumer Product Safety Act (CPSA), which aimed to "protect the public against unreasonable risks of injuries and deaths associated with consumer products." The CPSC began its operations a year later, in 1973. This organization administers the CPSA and the Consumer Product Safety Improvement Act of 2008 (CPSIA), as well as six other laws: the Federal Hazardous Substances Act, the Flammable Fabrics Act, the Poison Prevention

Packaging Act, the Refrigerator Safety Act, the Pool and Spa Safety Act, and the Children's Gasoline Burn Prevention Act.

The CPSC works to protect the public by:

1. Developing mandatory safety standards or banning consumer products if no feasible standard would adequately protect the public
2. Developing voluntary standards by working with relevant industries
3. Obtaining the recall of products that violate mandatory safety standards or pose a danger to consumer safety
4. Conducting research on potential product hazards
5. Conducting port surveillance and working with the governments of exporting countries to ensure that products entering the United States meet the standards set out by U.S. laws
6. Informing and educating consumers through the media, state and local governments, private organizations, and response to consumer inquiries

According to the CPSC, its efforts have "contributed significantly to the 30 percent decline in the rate of deaths and injuries associated with consumer products over the past 30 years."[1] In 2009, the CPSC had an operating budget of $108.2 million and a staff of 435 full-time equivalent employees, a substantial increase from its 2007 budget of $66.1 million and 393 full-time employees.[2] However, these increases are only a recent phenomenon as the resources of the CPSC declined until 2007 when the recalls pushed consumer product safety into the top of agenda for industry and regulators. Yet, despite the budget increase, staffing levels have yet to reach their previous numbers. For example, in 2004, the CPSC had a staff of 461, a number that was gradually reduced to 393 by 2007.

The CPSC collects information about product safety issues from hospitals, doctors, companies, newspaper reports, industry reports, consumer complaints, and investigations conducted by its staff. Federal law requires firms to report to the CPSC immediately (within 24 hours) after obtaining information that reasonably indicates a product contains a defect that creates a substantial risk of injury to the public, presents an unreasonable risk of serious injury or death, or violates a federal safety standard. Based on the information it receives, the CPSC then coordinates with the companies involved to recall the hazardous products from the market.

The CPSC receives an ever-increasing number of incident reports each year. For example, it received 50,000 incident reports in 2008, double the number it received in 2003. Unfortunately, due to inadequate staffing levels, the number of in-depth investigations conducted by the CPSC has remained stagnant over the years.

The cornerstone of the CPSC's philosophy is cooperation. When the CPSC receives information that a consumer product poses risk to users, it jointly investigates the issue with the company concerned in order to eliminate the hazard. Based on the investigation, the CPSC and the company mutually agree on a remedial action and announce the same. As a result, nearly all consumer product recalls in the United States are voluntary recalls. In some cases, the CPSC may issue a recall even when the firm does not cooperate, but such cases are extremely rare, occurring not more than once in the over four hundred recall campaigns conducted annually.

In the case of a hazardous product, remedial action would involve withdrawing the product from the market, either temporarily or permanently. A temporary withdrawal might involve repairing the product, usually by providing a retrofit repair kit to the consumers. For example, several strollers were recalled in 2009 for a potential amputation hazard. As part of the recall campaign, the company provided consumers with hinge covers, which made it impossible for children to place their fingers in the hinges.

A permanent withdrawal from the market involves remedial actions such as replacing or exchanging the product, refunding the purchase price, or instructing consumers to discard the product. For example, when RC2 issued a recall of toys due to excess lead in their surface paint, the company offered to provide its customers with a replacement toy.[3] Alternatively, when Target recalled dive sticks due to their risk as an impalement hazard, it offered to refund the purchase price.[4]

In certain circumstances in which it is not expedient to provide a repair and the product does not need to be returned to the seller, consumers may be asked to remove problematic components from the product in order to make it safe to use. For example, Evenflo sold about 25,000 telephone toys that had a mirror decal attached to them. When the company discovered that the decal could peel away and hence pose a choking hazard to children, it recalled these toys. As part of the recall, Evenflo simply asked consumers to remove the mirror decal from the toy and dispose of it.[5]

Occasionally, a recall may simply involve providing revised instructions. For example, EB Brands recalled about three million fitness balls in April 2009 because it received 47 reports of fitness balls unexpectedly bursting while they were being used, causing users to fall. As part of the recall campaign, EB Brands issued revised instructions that asked customers *not* to over-inflate the ball and *not* to use air compressors to inflate them.[6]

Regardless of the type of remedy provided and whether or not the product is withdrawn from the market, either temporarily or permanently, all such actions are considered recalls. In other words, a recall does not necessarily mean that consumers have to return the product to the seller. Also, a recall does not necessarily mean that the product itself is completely defective and unusable. A recall simply means that the product cannot be used in its original form. The extent of the modification required to make the product usable has no bearing on whether the action is termed a "recall" or not. Therefore, a recall may best be defined as "a formal request by a firm to its customers to discontinue the use of a product as it was sold or produced."

The CPSC oversees about 15,000 types of consumer products, from microwave ovens to cribs to lawn mowers. It organizes these products into six broad categories: children's products (not including toys), toys, household products, outdoor products, sports and recreation products, and specialty products. Each year, the CPSC issues over four hundred recalls, all of which fall within these six categories. For example, the CPSC issued 465 recalls in 2009, 563 in 2008, 472 in 2007, and 471 in 2006.

Hazards Leading to Injuries and Deaths

Based on its analysis of product defects that lead to recalls, the CPSC regularly identifies the "Top Five Hidden Home Hazards" and then lists them on its Web site in order to make consumers aware of exactly what these hazards are and how to avoid any related injuries. In 2007, the CPSC Web site identified the top five home hazards as: magnets, recalled products, tip-overs, windows and window coverings, and pool and spa drains. In addition, on an ongoing basis, the CPSC Web site identifies those recalled products it deems the most dangerous, highlighting them to ensure the recovery of such products. For example the Web site prominently displayed the following items as "CPSC's Most Wanted" in 2010: Playskool tool benches, Delta cribs (spring peg), Simplicity bassinets, Stork Craft cribs, MagnaMan figures, and Delta cribs (safety peg).

Judging from the hazards identified and the most-wanted list, it is clear that the CPSC places considerable emphasis on eliminating the dangers in products used by children. A wide range of consumer products present risks to children, including drowning in pools; choking and suffocation from toys; strangulation, suffocation, and entrapment in sleep environments; strangulation from window blind cords and clothing drawstrings; unintentional ingestion of toxic household chemicals; and various hazards from infant products such as cribs, high chairs, and strollers.

As figure 2.1 indicates, the number of toy-related injuries and deaths in the United States has been increasing over the years. The number of toy-related injuries has risen from 152,700 in 1994 to 253,300 in 2008, a 54 percent increase over a period of 15 years. After a record 255,100 toy-related injuries in 2001, the number dropped to 212,400 injuries the following year. However, since 2003, the number has been gradually increasing. Across all age groups, toy-related injuries have been increasing in a significant manner.

The number of toy-related deaths has also been increasing over the years. From 13 fatalities in 1997, the number of toy-related deaths more than doubled over the course of the next ten years, rising to 28 deaths in 2007. Although it appears that the number of deaths decreased to 19 in 2008, this total will likely be revised and increased as more accurate information about the causes of death becomes available in subsequent years. Analysis by the CPSC staff reveals that riding toys and choking are the two major causes of toy-related deaths.[7]

Because of rising toy-related dangers, the CPSC accords special attention to the issue of toy safety. Not surprisingly, more than half the CPSC staff (235 out of 435 staff members) is devoted to studying

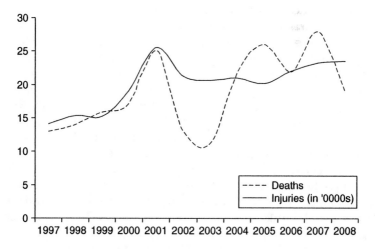

Figure 2.1   Toy-related injuries and deaths

and preventing hazards to children. An important step toward mini-mizing these injuries and deaths is to recall toys that pose a risk.

Toy Recalls Since 1990

All recalls issued by the CPSC are listed on the CPSC Web site (www. cpsc.gov). This Web site offers searchable information on over 4,500 recalls, based on product category, product type, company, product description, hazard type, and country/administrative area of manu-facture. In addition, the CPSC Web site also allows for searching by month, year, and press release number.

The very first recall in the toy category occurred on February 25, 1974, when the CPSC recalled 13,000 toy chests manufactured by Jackson Furniture Corporation[8] and sold by 40 different retailers. The recall occurred following the death of one child and a serious injury to another when these children's heads were caught between the front of the case and the lid of the chest. Before the recall was announced, production and sales were halted. Consumers who returned the chests received a refund of the full purchase price.

Following that first toy recall in 1974,[9] the CPSC went on to issue a total of 879 toy recalls by 2009. Of these, 169 recalls occurred before 1989. A number of recall notices in the earlier years did not have adequate information needed for analysis, likely because the CPSC was setting up systems and developing its own formats. Therefore, for the purposes of this book, only those recalls issued from 1990 onward have been considered, thereby avoiding issues that are no lon-ger relevant and may distort the picture. Further, since imports have increased during this study period (1990–2009), it provides a reason-able timeframe within which to examine issues related to recalls in the age of global business.

By extensively searching the CPSC Web site for toy recalls, a total of 710 recall notices issued over a period of two decades, between 1990 and 2009, were retrieved. Using the date of each recall announce-ment, all recalls that occurred during the period from 1990 to 2009 were counted in order to arrive at the annual figures.

As presented in figure 2.2, the steadily increasing number of toy recalls reached a historical peak of 83 recalls in 2007.[10] Not surpris-ingly, 2007 was dubbed the "Year of the Recall." Since then, however, recalls have been decreasing. Although recall numbers did remain high at 69 recalls in 2008, they went on to drop to 32 recalls in 2009. It may be noted that the years 2007 and 2008 witnessed the highest and second highest number of recalls. Of the total toy recalls that

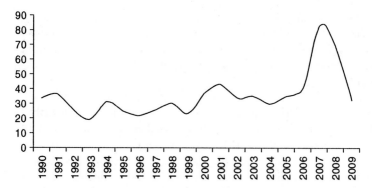

Figure 2.2   U.S. toy recalls (1990–2009)

occurred in the United States since 1990, 21.4 percent were issued in 2007 and 2008. If these years were typical, then the number of recalls issued would have been half those actually issued. In other words, both 2007 and 2008 were exceptional years for toy recalls.

Although the number of toy recalls decreased in 2009, the overall trend is clearly upward. For example, during the two decades studied (1990–2009), there was an average of 35.5 recalls each year. However, the average number of recalls for the first decade (1990–1999) was only 27, whereas for the second decade (2000–2009), it was 44. For the latest five-year period (2005–2009), the average number of recalls was 52, but it was only 27 for the corresponding period a decade ago (1995–1999). While recall numbers during the study period have increased, this growth has been quite irregular in nature. For example, from 1990 to 2009, the number of recalls had a standard deviation of 15.4, compared to the standard deviation during the first decade alone (1990–1999) of only 5.5, and that of the second decade alone (2000–2009), which was over three times higher at 17.7. The difference is even starker if the standard deviation of the latest five years is compared against the corresponding period a decade ago. During the period of 1995–1999, the standard deviation was only 3.1, but this figure increased to 22.7 during 2005–2009. In short, recalls have certainly increased overall, but they have done so erratically in the recent past.

Toy Recalls: Announcements versus Units

The foregoing analysis shows that toy recalls have increased in the recent past, but this trend must be understood in its proper perspective. An increase in the number of announcements does not necessarily mean that more toys are recalled; it simply means that toys are now recalled on more occasions. The increased number of recalls may be the result of prompt and proactive action by companies and regulators.

It is important to distinguish between recall announcements and recall size (i.e., the number of units) because recalls vary greatly with respect to the actual number of units recalled. For example, in 2008, Daiso issued a recall of stuffed toys made in Hong Kong, and in 2009, Edushape recalled Snap Beads made in China.[11] The reason for both recalls was a choking hazard, and in both cases, the number of units involved was only about 40 units. In a 2004 incident, the CPSC and four toy jewelry importers recalled 150 million units,[12] due to the fact that the toy jewelry, which was made in India, contained excess lead. Any analysis focusing only on the number of recalls issued will treat these three recalls as equal and might therefore conclude that there were more recalls in 2008 and 2009. However, in reality, the situation may have actually improved since 2004; fewer toys were involved in the recalls of Daiso and Edushape.

When a product poses a hazard, irrespective of the number of units involved, it should be recalled. Companies should not take chances, thinking that the issue only affects a small number of toys. At the same time, every recall should not be weighted in the same manner and with the assumption that things have gotten worse. Certainly, a recall involving a million units is more serious than a recall involving a hundred units.

If the increase in recalls involves a concomitant increase in the number of units recalled, the situation is more troubling. On the other hand, the picture is not as worrisome if, while more recalls are issued now, fewer toys are recalled in each case than in the past. The analysis in this section shows that, even though the number of recalls has increased, the actual number of toys recalled has not.

The CPSC's recall notices contain information about the number of units recalled. For analytical purposes, this information has been aggregated for each year between 1990 and 2009, during which over 370 million units of toys were recalled in 710 campaigns. Of these recalls, 38 accounted for over 311 million toys (about 84 percent of the total units). In other words, some recalls are clearly more severe than others since they involve more toys and affect more consumers.

While a few recalls account for a large number of units, many involved fewer units. For example, 268 recalls issued between 1990 and 2009 each involved 10,000 units or less. As a result, these 268 recalls accounted for a little over 1 million of the 370 million units recalled. Thus, nearly 38 percent of the recalls accounted for less than 0.3 percent of the total units recalled. This example indicates that focusing only on the number of recalls can result in a very skewed understanding of the phenomenon. Therefore, it is important to examine not only the number of recalls but the number of units recalled each year.

The best way to understand whether the number of units recalled has increased, is to examine the average recall size, that is, the number of toys recalled in a given year divided by the number of recalls issued that year. It is clear (from figure 2.2 earlier) that recalls have increased recently. If the average recall size has also increased, then the data point to a disturbing trend in which more recalls are issued, more products are involved, and hence, more consumers are affected.

Figure 2.3 shows that, barring a few exceptions (such as 2004 and 1999), recall size has been decreasing since 2000. In fact, at over 204,541 units, the average recall size for the period of 2005–2009 is the lowest to date. This trend is particularly revealing if the average recall size of 2005–2009 is compared with the average recall size of a decade before (1995–1999), which stood at over 610,000 units and was nearly three times the average recall size for 2005–2009. In short, while recalls have increased in the recent years, many of these recalls involved considerably fewer units. For example, a record 33 "small" recalls (involving 10,000 units or less) were issued in 2008. Of these, 10 involved 500 units or less. As a result, although 69 recalls (the

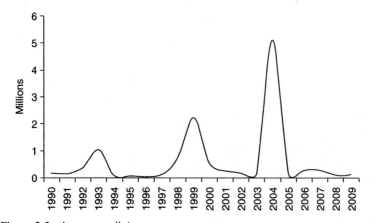

Figure 2.3 Average recall size

second highest number) were issued in 2008, the average recall size was the lowest in the recent past.

What is most interesting in figure 2.3 is the average recall size for 2007. Previously, figure 2.2 showed that the number of recall announcements peaked in 2007. However, when considering recall size, 2007 appears to be a normal year. In fact, of the 83 recalls issued in 2007, nearly 39 percent (32 recalls) involved 10,000 units or less. In other words, although 2007 was dubbed the "Year of the Recall," things were not as bad as they appeared: many of the recalls involved fewer units.

While figure 2.3 reduces the concern about 2007, it also points to three years that should be viewed as abnormal: 1993, 1999, and 2004. Of the three, 2004 stands out as particularly exceptional since it recorded the highest number of toys recalled in any year (153.4 million units). Of these, two recalls accounted for 151 million units—one involving 150 million pieces of toy jewelry and another involving one million children's rings.[13] Both products were made in India and both were recalled for excess lead. Although only half of these toys actually had excess lead, it was logistically impossible to verify which of the products posed a risk and which did not. Therefore, the companies and the CPSC recalled all the toys and advised consumers to discard them.

Similar to the 2004 recall of toy jewelry, recalls in 1999 were also notable—nearly 51.7 million toys recalled that year. There were two very large recalls: The first was a Burger King recall of 25 million Pokémon balls that posed a suffocation hazard to children under three years of age, even though the packaging described them as being safe for children of all ages. The recall aimed to take the balls away from children under three years of age, who are more prone to suffocation hazards. The second case involved 15 firms recalling 19 million dive sticks because they posed a previously unrecognized impalement hazard. As a result, the recall included all diving sticks sold over the course of several years.[14] Thus, the number of units recalled in some years may be much higher in some cases because it was simply infeasible to distinguish the defective products from safe products, previously unknown hazards became apparent, or new regulations may have come into force.

In short, the number of recalls has been increasing in recent years; however, many of these appear to be small recalls involving fewer units. While an increase in the number of recalls is a matter of concern, the situation would be even more serious if there had been a similar increase in the number of units recalled. The increase in recalls could be a result of the CPSC becoming increasingly diligent in its role as a product safety watchdog or simply because certain issues have become more salient in recent years. In order to understand the actual reasons for the increase in recalls, one must understand the nature of recalls.

Rising Recalls but Fewer Explanations

The increase in recalls has spurred several explanations and theories as to what is causing them. First and foremost, we must examine China's unique position within the issue. Several analysts have noted that toy manufacturing shifted largely to China, particularly since 2001, following the country's accession to the World Trade Organization. As the sociopolitical and regulatory environment in China is different from that in the developed world, critics have argued that the quality of manufacturing is poor, leading to increased recalls. For example, Yadong Luo suggests that moral degradation occurred in China following its exposure to and experiment with capitalism.[15] He posits that organizations without the necessary control systems in place are likely to face quality issues arising from the opportunistic behavior of the Chinese suppliers.

Others have also offered moral degradation and opportunism as an explanation, but with a different twist. Jay Barney and Shujun Zhang suggest that China has developed a reputation for good quality at an affordable price, and that some players in the industry may try to free-ride on this reputation by providing low-quality goods, which in turn leads to recalls and endangers Brand China.[16]

Yet another explanation scholars offer relates to the cost pressures Chinese suppliers face. Some argue that rapid industrialization has resulted in substantial cost increases in China. As the multinational corporations and big-box retailers pressure Chinese suppliers to supply products at ever-lower prices, the suppliers resort to cutting corners, which compromises the quality of the manufacturing.[17]

The nature and length of supply chains in China has also been offered as an explanation for the increase in recalls. It is well known that supply chains in China are quite long and complex, encompassing a web of contractual and subcontractual relationships. As a result, a problem at one end of the supply chain may become larger, due to a ripple effect, and may in turn result in poor quality in a large number of products. These problems will be even more acute in supply chain relationships that are characterized by a low level of trust and limited understanding of on-the-ground realities in China.[18]

Another argument is that the massive growth in China has meant that skilled workers, managers, and entrepreneurs are in short supply. Further, as this growth has continued, those with little or no knowledge of operations have assumed critical roles that they were not ready for in the business and manufacturing arena, causing quality to suffer and recalls to increase.

These explanations, all of which center on China, fall short in a number of ways. First, China is not the only developing country that makes products intended for consumption in the United States and elsewhere. Other countries, including India, Indonesia, the Philippines, Vietnam, and Thailand also face problems such as inadequate regulatory systems, moral hazards, opportunism, lack of skilled human resources, and complex supply chains. But, for reasons that are unclear, the products from these countries are not the ones cited for poor quality and recalls. If these same factors have resulted in poor-quality products made in other countries as well, then the focus on China as the sole culprit certainly seems to be misplaced.

Second, China is often referred to as the "Workshop of the World." The reality is that Chinese factories, while certainly important, are only one component of the global supply chains. These products are designed and engineered in one country, but their components are sourced, produced, and tested in many others before they are marketed globally. Therefore, focusing only on China reveals only a partial picture.

Finally, a number of explanations surrounding China's issues with product quality are offered without any empirical support. While some of these explanations may in fact be plausible, they have very little empirical evidence to back the argument that China is delivering poor quality products and, thus, causing recalls. Certainly the research on product recalls involving China is riddled with a number of sensational anecdotes,[19] but this information might not reflect the actual trend. Therefore, it is important to examine the nuances of the data related to recalls in order to get a better overall perspective on product safety and recalls. This book aims to do exactly that. Toward that purpose, the next chapter seeks to answer the question: Have recalls of Chinese-made toys really increased in the recent years?

Chapter 3

Toy Recalls and China: The Twain that Always Meet?

As we have already established, toy recalls have increased over the recent past, and several explanations for this trend have revolved around China. The toy industry is very global in nature, involving several multinational corporations, worldwide supply chains, and a global market. However, over two-thirds of all toys sold in the world are made in China. Therefore, when toy recalls occur, it is likely that the recalled products are made in China, and thus, it is common to suspect that Chinese manufacturing practices are to blame.

Recalls of Toys Made in China

The CPSC recall notices provide information about where a toy has been manufactured, and this information can be used to count the number of recalls involving toys made in China to see whether recalls of toys made in China have increased in the recent years. Figure 3.1 depicts the number of recalls of Chinese-made toys against all the toy recalls issued in the United States. During the period of 1990–2009, toys made in China were recalled on 418 separate occasions, constituting nearly 59 percent of the 710 toy recalls issued in the United States during the same period.

Figure 3.1 shows that the number of recalls involving toys made in China remained low and fairly stable until 1999. Between 1990 and 1999, Chinese-made toys were recalled at an average of 10 times a year, with the number of Chinese-made toy recalls during this period never exceeding 20. In fact, the number of recalls of Chinese-made toys was in single digits for half that period. Recalls involving

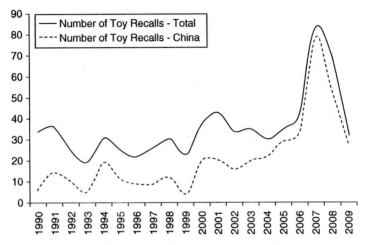

Figure 3.1   Toy recalls—total versus China

Chinese-made toys during the period of 1990–1999 represented only 37 percent of the total, 99 of the 271 issued.

But Chinese-made toy recalls have been rising since 2000. During the period of 2000–2009, Chinese-made toys were recalled at an average of 32 times a year. The number of recalls involving Chinese-made toys during this period stood at 319 out of the total 439 issued, about 73 percent of all recalls. Hence, we can see that the proportion of Chinese-made toy recalls doubled compared to the previous decade.

The increase in Chinese-made toy recalls in the latest decade is even more telling when comparing the latest five year period (2005–2009) against the same period a decade ago (1995–1999). In the latest five-year period, Chinese-made toys were recalled at an average 44 times per year, in contrast to 9 times per year during 1995–1999. During 2005–2009, about 85 percent of all U.S. toy recalls involved those made in China, whereas only 36 percent of toy recalls involved China during 1995–1999.

The increase in recalls of toys made in China compared to recalls of toys made elsewhere is telling. The recalls of toys made in China have risen dramatically since 2002. During the same period, however, the recalls of toys made elsewhere have decreased. Surprisingly, in 2008, the recalls of toys made elsewhere increased to 17, before dropping to 5 in the following year. The countries inolved in toy recalls in 2008 included Hong Kong (5), Taiwan (3), India (3), Thailand (2), Indonesia (1), Trinidad (1), Germany (1), and the United States (1).

The sudden rise in the recalls of toys made outside China not only reflects the shifting of some toy manufacturing out of China following the recalls crisis in 2007 but also indicates that such moves alone may not decrease recalls in the United States.

It is obvious that the number of recalls of Chinese-made toys has increased, but it is also important to examine the recall size (number of toys recalled) in order to understand whether manufacturing problems in China have led to large recall numbers. If all of these recalls involved large numbers of units, thus affecting a large number of consumers, public outrage against China is quite understandable.

From 1990 to 2009, a total of 371.1 million toys were recalled in the United States, and of these, 90.4 million toys were made in China. In other words, nearly a quarter of the toys recalled in the United States since 1990 were made in China. This fraction of toys accounted for about 59 percent of total recall announcements, which suggests that while recalls of Chinese-made toys did occur more frequently, they did not involve large numbers of toys.

In any analysis, it is important to note the exceptions and see whether they have influenced the pattern. As discussed in chapter 2, a 2004 recall of toy jewelry involved 150 million units. The recalled jewelry contained excessive lead and was made in India. This single recall constituted 40 percent of all the toys recalled in the United States during 1990–2009. It would seem likely that this recall should have decreased the percentage of China-made toys recalled, but, in fact, that does not appear to be the case. Excluding this recall of 150 million units, the toys made in China represented only 40 percent of the total toys recalled. So, proportionately, made-in-China recall announcements should have been around 40 percent of the total, but were in fact about 59 percent. Hence, while the number of recalls involving Chinese-made toys was indeed higher, this statistic did not necessarily translate into affecting a larger number of people since the recalls were often very small and involved relatively few units.

While Chinese-made toy recalls have not always involved large numbers, the number of Chinese-made toys recalled in the recent past has been increasing. During 1990–1999, only 6.4 million out of the 123.6 million toys recalled (about 5 percent) were made in China. However, 83.9 million out of the 247.5 million toys recalled (about 34 percent) during 2000–2009 were made in China. If the 2004 recall of 150 million pieces of toy jewelry is excluded, the proportion of Chinese-made toys in the total number of toys recalled during 2000–2009 stands at about 86 percent, which is likely more representative of the real situation. The fact that about 89 percent of the toys recalled during 2005–2009 were made in China supports the conclusion about an increase in Chinese-made toys recalls.

During 2007, a notable year for recalls, 23.5 million toys made in China were recalled. Continuing this trend, nearly seven million Chinese-made toys were recalled in 2008. The figure dropped to 2.1 million in 2009, China's second lowest recall size in the 2000s. Although it is difficult to tell whether this decrease is random or somewhat systematic, it is nevertheless welcome.

In sum, there have been more recalls of Chinese-made toys in the 2000s, but these did not necessarily involve greater numbers of toys. However, the number of Chinese-made toys recalled has also been increasing in the last few years. This increase in recalls of Chinese-made toys and number of units involved does not necessarily mean that China is the source of the recalls. Rather, the increase may simply be due to increased toy imports from China.[1] In other words, it is likely that an increase in Chinese-made toy recalls is simply due to more toys being imported from China. The following sections examine this possibility.

U.S. International Trade and Toys

The value of U.S. imports in 2008 was over $2 trillion, over four times their value in 1990. In contrast, U.S. exports accounted for $1.28 trillion in 2008, which was more than three times the value of exports in 1990. In 2008, total U.S. trade figures stood at $3.4 trillion, a fourfold increase since 1990. The majority (52.1 percent) of U.S. international trade was conducted with five trading partners: Canada (16.4 percent), China (14 percent), Mexico (11.7 percent), Japan (5.6 percent), and Germany (4.4 percent).

In the early 1990s, U.S. imports exceeded U.S. exports by about $100 billion. But a decade later, U.S. imports exceeded U.S. exports by about $500 billion, reaching a whopping $816.2 billion difference in 2008. These figures tell us that consumption in the United States has become heavily dependent on imports. This upward shift can be clearly observed in figure 3.2, which presents total U.S. international trade figures (both imports and exports) for our study period. Although the data used for analysis in this section includes the figures for 2009, this data will likely be subject to revision as clearer information becomes available.[2] Therefore, any trends or analysis related to 2009 must be treated with caution.

As figure 3.2 indicates, U.S. international trade has increased substantially over the last two decades. The growth of exports, however,

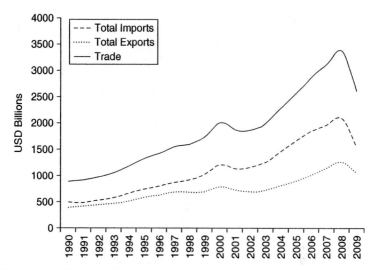

Figure 3.2 U.S. international trade

has been relatively low compared to that of imports, which have risen dramatically, particularly in the 2000s. The majority (55.5 percent) of U.S. imports arrived from five countries: China (19 percent), Canada (14.4 percent), Mexico (11.3 percent), Japan (6.2 percent), and Germany (4.6 percent). In fact, nearly a third of U.S. imports were from China and Canada alone. Interestingly, although Canada is the United States' largest trading partner, imports from China were higher than those from Canada. This change in the pattern of imports from Canada and China is itself revealing (see figure 3.3). Clearly, China's low-cost manufacturing advantage has proved formidable and difficult to compete with, even for Canada, which enjoys a special geographic, political, and economic relationship with the United States. As a result, Canada's share of U.S. imports has been falling, while the Chinese share has been rising dramatically.

In 1990, imports from China accounted for about 3.1 percent of total U.S. imports. In contrast, imports from Canada represented about 18.5 percent. In the 1990s, imports from Canada rose marginally, but gradually, and reached 19.6 percent of total imports in 1996. However, since 2000, imports from Canada have been decreasing steadily, falling to 16.1 percent in 2008. In contrast, imports from China have risen with each passing year, overtaking Canadian imports in 2007. In 2009, imports from China accounted for 19 percent of total imports to United States, whereas the imports from

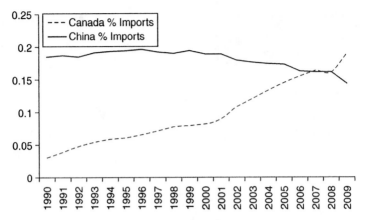

Figure 3.3   U.S. imports from China and Canada

Canada stood at 14.4 percent. In other words, while imports from Canada declined during the last two decades, imports from China increased nearly six-fold during that same period. As a result, China has become the primary source of imports to the United States, relegating Canada to second position.

The United States imports a wide variety of products from China, including nearly all imaginable electrical, electronic, and mechanical goods used by households and businesses. In addition, several food products, ranging from fish to dairy products to beverages, are imported from China. Table 3.1 presents the top 10 Chinese imports, from computers to apparel. However, while electronic items like computers, televisions, and telecommunications may be assembled in China, their component parts are often sourced from various companies in other countries. For example, Apple's iPod touch is assembled and tested in China, but not all of its most expensive components are made in China or by Chinese companies. Toshiba (Japanese company) makes the iPod's hard drive in China; Toshiba-Matsushita makes its display module in Japan; Broadcom (U.S. company) makes its video/multimedia processor in Taiwan or Singapore; PortalPlayer (U.S. company) makes its portal player CPU in the United States or Taiwan; Renesas (Japanese company) makes its display driver in Japan; and Samsung (Korean company) makes the iPod's mobile SDRAM memory in Korea.[3]

An abundance of human resources has helped China specialize in labor-intensive products and labor-intensive activities. Not surprisingly, Chinese-made toys, apparel, footwear, and furniture are among

Table 3.1 Top 10 imported products from China

(Value in Million Dollars)

Product Category	2005	2006	2007	2008	2009
Computers	14,453	17,371	23,240	25,040	28,299
Other (clocks, port typewriters, other household) goods	22,654	26,547	27,548	27,505	27,081
Toys, shooting and sporting goods, and bicycles	20,160	22,208	27,583	29,167	25,094
Computer accessories, peripherals, and parts	25,746	28,931	28,093	27,012	22,071
Television receivers, VCR's, and other video equipment	10,755	14,542	12,907	15,105	15,084
Apparel and household goods (cotton)	7,618	9,872	13,004	13,382	14,446
Apparel and household goods (other textiles)	13,104	14,590	15,809	15,295	14,381
Telecommunications equipment	7,022	8,659	12,569	14,497	11,778
Furniture, household items, baskets	11,546	13,198	13,949	13,279	10,997
Footwear of leather, rubber, or other materials	9,631	10,700	11,163	11,632	10,969

Source: U.S. Census Bureau, Foreign Trade Division.

the products most imported into the United States. In fact, China has become the main source for a number of products consumed globally. Most prominent among these are toys, a category in which China dominates. Nearly two-thirds of the toys sold in the world are made in China.

Nearly 95 percent of all toys sold in the United States are imported from other countries. Over the years, China has become a major source of these toys. In turn, toys have become an important component of China's trade, as they represent about six percent of total Chinese exports to the United States. Overall imports of toys by the United States have increased from about $7 billion in 1992 to over $20 billion in 2009 (see figure 3.4). Imports of toys specifically from China have increased from about $3 billion in 1992 to over $20 billion in 2008, before dropping to $18.3 billion in 2009.

Chinese-made toys accounted for nearly 90 percent of toy imports to the United States in 2009, up dramatically from about 41 percent in 1992. China's rise has come at the expense of other toy-exporting countries, whose combined share of toy imports to the U.S. market plummeted from 59 percent to 10 percent during the same period.

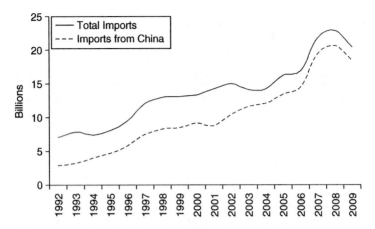

Figure 3.4   U.S. toy imports—total versus China

For instance, Japan remained a strong exporter of toys to the United States until a substantial drop occurred around 2001. Despite the benefit of geographical proximity, Mexico has not been able to sustain the uptick it experienced in 2002. As for Taiwan and Hong Kong, their toy exports to the United States have both been declining for over a decade.[4]

Interestingly, toy imports from China seem to have increased despite the spate of recalls in 2007. In 2008, toy imports from China increased by 1.3 percent, reaching a historic high of $20.7 billion. In 2009, the value of toy imports into the United States decreased by 10.5 percent overall, but imports from China decreased by less than 1 percent, remaining at $18.3 billion. In short, China continues to be the major source of toy imports and meets nearly 85 percent of U.S. demand for toys.[5] The question is whether the increased recalls of Chinese-made toys are simply a reflection of increased imports from China or whether they are disproportionate to China's share of toy imports to the United States.

Chinese Recall Proportions vis-a-vis Imports

Figure 3.5 examines whether the recalls of Chinese-made toys are proportionate to the number of toys imported from China. It depicts toy imports from China as a percentage of total U.S. toy imports and recalls of toys made in China as a percentage of U.S. toy recalls.

The percentage of Chinese-made toy recalls has exceeded the percentage of Chinese toy imports on only three occasions since

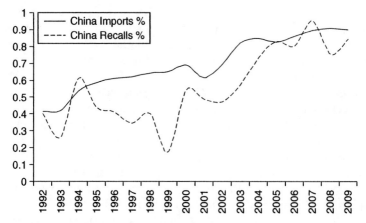

Figure 3.5   Growth in Chinese imports and recalls

1992: in 1994 (by 7.7 percent), in 2005 (by 0.12 percent), and in 2007 (by 5.85 percent). Between 1992 and 2009, recalls of Chinese-made toys were about 14 percent lower than the percentage of Chinese toys in U.S. imports. However, during the period of 2000–2009, this figure decreased to about 11 percent. For the latest five years in our study period (2005–2009), the recalls of Chinese-made toys were lower than the percentage of Chinese toy imports by only 4 percent. The best example, perhaps, is 2009, when toy imports from China accounted for 89.75 percent of U.S. toy imports, and 84.38 percent of U.S. toy recalls involved toys made in China. In other words, while the recalls of Chinese-made toys have generally been low proportionate to the imports of toys from China, recalls have still been increasing dramatically in the recent past.

Although, for purposes of brevity, we have not presented this information in figure 3.5, we must point out that the percentage of Chinese-made toys recalled (reflecting the size of the recall) during our study period was lower than the percentage of Chinese toy imports. But, during 1992–2009, the percentage of Chinese-made toys recalled was higher than the percentage of imports from China on six occasions. The extent to which the number of recalled Chinese-made toys exceeded the percentage of imports from China ranged from about 6 percent in 1994 to about 19 percent in 2001. Hence, the trend presented in figure 3.5 (using recalls of Chinese-made toys as a percentage) largely holds true for the number of toys recalled as well.

In sum, U.S. recalls of toys made in China have definitely been increasing, particularly in the recent past. Despite the large number of recalls of Chinese-made toys, the number of toys involved in them have generally been low. But, even the number of units of recalled Chinese-made toys has been increasing in the recent years, which raises a concern about the quality of Chinese products. However, when the increase of Chinese-made toy recalls is compared to the increase in toy imports from China, a somewhat different picture emerges. Generally, recalls of Chinese-made toys as a percentage of total U.S. toy recalls are lower relative to the percentage of Chinese toy imports in total toy imports to United States. However, even if they are lower than the percentage of toy imports from China, it is a matter of concern that the proportions of Chinese-made toy recalls have been increasing in the last few years. While many have offered explanations as to why there has been an increase in recalls of Chinese-made products, a dominant explanation relates to price and cost pressures. So the question is: Have cost pressures increased recalls of toys made in China?

Chapter 4

China's Toy Recalls: The High Cost of Low Price?

A common assumption is that product recalls are directly related to low prices, that is, low-priced products are typically recalled because they lack quality. Several analysts argue that manufacturers in the developing world, particularly in China, habitually offer a low price and good samples in order to win contracts. After that point, however, these manufacturers change their specifications and substitute cheaper materials or generally compromise on quality. These arguments imply that suppliers in the developing world, particularly in China, are simply corrupt. Others, however, argue that suppliers compromise quality due to the ever-increasing pressure to supply goods at lower prices.

Each of these arguments—suppliers in China are corrupt or they are forced to compromise quality due to cost pressures—is verifiable only through anecdotes or in-depth case studies. Findings from such studies, however, may not be generalizable. One way to test these arguments using large scale, objective data might be to analyze the recalls by price of the recalled product. Such an analysis assumes that cost pressures are likely to be highest for low-priced products and that the manufacturers of high-priced products are likely to enjoy some cushion, which prevents them from compromising quality to protect future business. In other words, there is a higher chance that companies and contract manufacturers that sell low-priced products will compromise on quality because the margins in such products are razor thin. Therefore, if the majority of products recalled are at the lower end of the price spectrum, one can infer that cost pressures—and likely, corruption—are playing a role. On the other hand, if the majority of products recalled fall on the higher end of the price spectrum, one can assume that different factors are involved.

Recalls of Low- and High-Priced Toys

The CPSC recall notices indicate the price at which a recalled toy has been sold. For example, the notice announcing a recall of toy guns by Dollar General indicates that the items sold for about $5 per unit.[1] The notices do not always indicate a single price, but rather a price range. For example, the notice announcing Weight Watchers' recall of plush Hungry Figures and Hungry Magnets indicates that these toys were sold for between $4 and $7, which comes to an average price of $5.50.[2] Such price information can be used to examine whether there has been an increase in recalls of low-priced toys.

For the purposes of this study, $10 was chosen as a divider between low- and high-priced toys. During the study period of 1990–2009, there were 350 recalls involving toys priced at $10 or less. This category also involved some free promotional toys. In contrast, 327 recalls involved toys that sold for more than $10. In other words, the $10 price point separates the sample approximately into two halves. Accordingly, low-priced toys were those sold for $10 or less while high-priced toys were those that sold for over $10. Figure 4.1 presents the yearly aggregates according to this classification.

As shown in figure 4.1, more of the recalls in the 2000s involved high-priced products than low-priced products. But there is an interesting trend. During the 1990s, low-priced toys were recalled more frequently than high-priced toys. This trend remained consistent throughout the decade, then reversed in the 2000s, when more

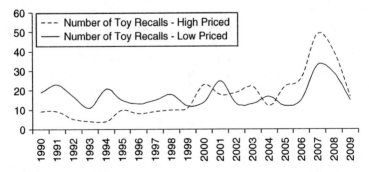

Figure 4.1   Number of low- and high-priced toy recalls

recalls involved high-priced toys. In fact, there were more recalls of high-priced toys in every year of the 2000s, except in 2001 and 2004. Interestingly, the numbers of low-priced toy recalls appear to have remained somewhat stable, whereas the numbers of high-priced toy recalls appear to be rising. For example, during the 1990s, low-priced toys were recalled at an average of 16 times per year, while there were only half as many recalls of high-priced toys, an average of 8 per year. However, during the 2000s, high-priced toys were recalled at an average 25 times per year—much more frequently than the average of 19 recalls for low-priced toys and three times more often than in the previous decade. The contrast is even starker for the latest five year period alone (2005–2009), during which low-priced toys were recalled 21 times per year on average, but high-priced toys were recalled about 31 times per year—about 50 percent more often.

The reversal is even more evident when these recalls are analyzed as proportions of total toy recalls. Toys sold at $10 and under constituted about 60 percent of the recalls during 1990s, whereas those sold at over $10 represented only 27 percent of the recalls for that same time period, on average.[3] Low-priced toys were recalled twice as many times as high-priced toys during this period. Then, during the 2000s, this picture changed. About 43 percent of recalls involved toys that sold for $10 or less, and 55 percent of recalls involved toys that sold for over $10. Hence, the number of recalls of toys priced at over $10 nearly doubled in the 2000s, compared to the figures from the 1990s.

The last five years of study period (2005–2009) indicate that the proportion of high-priced toy recalls may be decreasing, while that for low-priced toys is increasing. This could signal early evidence of cost pressures having an effect, or it could simply be a random reversal. Nevertheless, even during this period, the absolute numbers and proportions of recalls involving toys over $10 remain higher than those involving toys sold for $10 and under.

The calculations presented in figure 4.1 include U.S. recalls of toys made in all countries. It is likely that, due to high demand levels, cost pressures affect Chinese manufactures more than manufacturers in other countries. If this is truly the case, then the number of low-priced recalls and their proportions in all toy recalls should be increasing for China. At the same time, the number of low-priced recalls and their proportions in all toy recalls should be decreasing or remaining steady for toys made elsewhere.

Recalls of Low- and High-Priced Toys Made in China and Elsewhere

Low-priced toys figured prominently in total recalls, but high-priced recalls were also common (please refer to figure 4.1). However, price-based analysis of recalls reveals a somewhat different picture for toys made in China. Nearly all recalls of Chinese-made toys during the 1990s involved low-priced items (perhaps because only low-priced products were imported from China during that period). In the 2000s, nearly all toy production shifted from the United States to China; since then, recalls of high-priced toys have increased, surpassing those of low-priced toys in 2003. In subsequent years, with the exception of 2004, high-priced toy recalls were more frequent than low-priced recalls.

During the 1990s, recalls of high-priced toys made in China occurred at a marginal rate of once per year, whereas low-priced toys were recalled eight times on average per year. In the next decade (2000–2009), recalls of high-priced toys increased to an average of 15 per year; the number for low-priced toys increased to 14 per year. The latest five years (2005–2009) show an even greater contrast, with recalls of Chinese-made, high-priced toys occurring at an average of 24 times per year, while Chinese-made, low-priced toys were recalled at an average of 14 times per year. In short, while recalls of both low- and high-priced toys made in China have increased over the years, recalls of high-priced toys increased much more than did those of low-priced toys.

Examining the trends of low-priced toy recalls as a subset of toys made in China may not provide a complete picture because there is no reference point for comparison. Comparing recalls of low-priced toys made in China with those of toys made elsewhere provides a more accurate representation. Figure 4.2 plots the recalls of low-priced toys as a percentage of recalls of toys made in China and elsewhere.[4]

From figure 4.2, it appears that despite occasional fluctuations, recalls of low-priced toys made in China (as a percentage of recalls of all toys made in China) have been decreasing over the years. However, since 2007, the proportion of low-priced toys among Chinese recalls seems to have been consistently increasing, albeit somewhat marginally. In contrast, the percentage of low-priced toys among recalls of toys made outside China has decreased sharply between 1990 and 2005, save for occasional fluctuations. But since 2005, the proportion of low-priced toys in recalls of toys made elsewhere appears to be on the rise. This trend since 2005—evident only for this

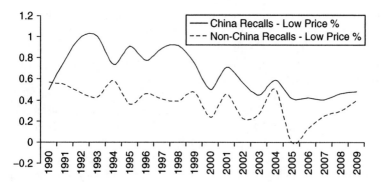

Figure 4.2   Proportion of low-priced toy recalls in recalls of toys made in China and elsewhere

period—shows that low-priced toys made outside China are more likely to be defective.

It must be noted that, even with the increase in recalls of low-priced toys made outside China, their proportion remains within the historical range of low-priced toys recalled. Also, given that very few toys imported to the United States are now made outside China, these numbers represent considerably fewer toy recalls in absolute numbers, as evidenced by the fact that there were only nine recalls of low-priced toys ($10 and under) made outside China during 2005–2009. For example, there were five recalls of low-priced toys made outside China in 2008, the highest number in recent years. Of these, two involved toys made in Hong Kong, two involved toys made in Taiwan, and one was related to toys made in India.

In short, the analysis in this chapter shows that recalls of high-priced toys have been increasing. This increase is true for toys made in China and elsewhere. Furthermore, there also seems to be an increase—albeit marginal—in recalls of low-priced toys in recent years. These findings test the conventional wisdom that recalls of low-priced toys are more frequent and, even more importantly, raise questions about the notion that cost pressures on and opportunistic behavior by Chinese suppliers have resulted in an increase in toy recalls.

The above analysis assumed that cost pressures would likely be higher at the low-priced end of the market. In making a low-priced toy, each of the involved parties must adhere to the low-price philosophy and operate on a tight budget. If there is any scope for *not* meeting the performance requirements, some party involved in the manufacturing might compromise quality by substituting the materials or changing the specifications. In such cases, recalls would be likely to occur, if not completely inevitable. Therefore, this method is a fairly reasonable approach to use in examining whether cost pressures have indeed resulted in higher recalls in the recent past.

This chapter's analysis categorizes toys as either low- or high-priced, based on the criteria of a $10 sales price. Some might question this criteria since "$10 and under" may not, in fact, be an accurate representation of a "low price." Even so, this was the most conservative estimate; therefore, if cost pressures had any effect, it would have shown up more clearly in the $10-and-under category. Further, the $10 mark separates the recalls approximately into halves. A figure like $20 categorizes nearly 75 percent of all recalls as low-priced, thus making it impossible to achieve a meaningful comparison between the two sets.

The analysis in this chapter does not reveal whether or not cost pressures do in fact exist. It merely tests whether cost pressures might have resulted in recalls. In doing so, this analysis assumes that cost pressures are more likely to be higher at the lower end of the market, causing quality to be compromised in low-priced products, which would then lead to recalls. In other words, cost pressures at the lower end mean that the number of recalls at the lower end would be higher and would increase rapidly.

The data presented in the figures in this chapter consider the number of recalls only, not recall size. However, the trends were similar, even for recall size. In other words, a greater number of high-priced toys have been recalled in the recent past, and this fact is even more likely to hold true for toys made in China, as the number of high-priced toys recalled has increased in the latest decade of the study period (2000–2009).

In sum, contrary to common assumptions, recalls of low-priced toys appear to be decreasing over the years. Alternatively, recalls of low-priced toys have been increasing at a lower rate compared to high-priced toys. If cost pressures are a real factor, then low-priced toys should have appeared in more recalls than high-priced toys. Also, the low-priced toy recalls should have increased at a faster pace than high-priced toy recalls. Instead, the trend shows that recalls of low-priced toys have increased, but at a slower rate than those of high-priced toys. Also, the proportion of low-priced toys in recalls has decreased over time, particularly in the recent past, which raises the question of whether cost pressures are indeed resulting in poor quality.

In order to derive a reasonable conclusion about the role of Chinese manufacturers in recalls, one must examine the nature of the flaws that have resulted in recalls. Answering this question requires a closer examination of the toy industry and the operation of global supply chains. Chinese manufacturers are largely responsible for manufacturing, not designing, toys. Hence, if Chinese manufacturers have been compromising quality, this would be reflected in more recalls of toys for manufacturing problems. The analysis in the next chapter examines this issue by asking: Have recalls increased due to manufacturing flaws in Chinese-made toys?

Chapter 5

Toys Made in China, but Designed in...?

The previous chapters have highlighted the fact that toy recalls have been increasing over time, particularly for those made in China. The latter increase, however, is congruent with the corresponding rise in imports from China. Contrary to speculations that these recalls are occurring due to cost pressures, the data show that, in the recent past, recalls of high-priced toys have increased faster than recalls of low-priced toys, particularly for toys made in China. If low-priced toy recalls had increased, that would have been a reasonable indication of Chinese manufacturers compromising on quality. However, the absence of an increase in low-priced toy recalls does not clearly establish that there are no cost pressures. It is possible that, within Chinese manufacturing as a whole, problems may exist that simply affect products across the price spectrum. One way to examine this is to study whether the recalls occurred mainly due to poor manufacturing practices in general.

When examining recalls, it is important to take into account the nature of global supply chains. While a large number of toys are made in China, these toys are often made according to design specifications of toy companies headquartered elsewhere. Not surprisingly, in recall crisis situations, Chinese officials and suppliers claim they are not at fault and that they made the products according to the design specifications of the brand-owning companies. If manufacturing practices are responsible for recalls, then a larger number of recalls would be for manufacturing flaws. If Chinese manufacturing practices in particular are at fault, there would be an increase in recalls for flawed manufacturing in the 2000s, coinciding with the shift of manufacturing to China. On the other hand, if recalls due to design flaws are higher and increasing, Chinese manufacturing alone cannot be held responsible for the rise in recalls. This chapter studies the nature of toy recalls to determine whether those specifically due to manufacturing problems have increased in the recent past. To better appreciate the importance of distinguishing between manufacturing and design flaws, one must first understand the global nature of toy supply chains and the role of Chinese factories within them.

Global Nature of Toy Supply Chains

Traditionally, companies have traded goods and services across borders. An across-the-border transaction means that an imported product has been designed and produced in a single country with material from that country. However, growth in information technology and falling transportation costs have increased trade in the areas of tasks and components. As Gene Grossman and Esteban Rossi-Hansberg succinctly state (in reference to David Ricardo's theory on international trade), "It's not wine for cloth anymore." In fact, trade in tasks and components characterizes the global supply chains of today. For example, Mattel's Barbie is designed in the United States, but it uses plastic from Taiwan, hair from Japan, and cloth from China. Workers assemble it in Indonesia and Malaysia. Further, quality testing and marketing—two very important tasks—are performed both in the United States and around the world.[1] This shows that global supply chains are complex, but it still does not provide the complete story, since the picture changes continuously, as multinational corporations constantly seek cheaper and better sources for the components and tasks that go into making their products.

The globalization of supply chains is particularly evident in the toy industry, which was estimated to be a $78.1 billion business in the year 2008, a slight decline from $78.7 billion 2007,[2] largely due to the falling value of the U.S. dollar. If the 2008 market is valued at the 2007 U.S.-dollar rate, the global toy market can be estimated at about $80.5 billion, that is, an increase of about 2.3 percent. Using this figure, we can see that although the dollar value of the global toy market appears to have declined from 2007 to 2008, the volume of toys sold likely increased.

The top five toy markets in 2008 were the United States, Japan, China, the United Kingdom, and France. Together, these five countries account for 51.4 percent of toy sales around the world. The United States alone accounts for about 28 percent of the global market, with an average of $281 spent annually on each child. In contrast, in China, which accounts for 5.8 percent of the global toy market, consumers spend $17 annually on toys per child. In India, that figure is only $5.

While the major markets for toys exist in the United States and Europe, toy production is concentrated in Asia, and primarily in China. It is estimated that about 60 percent of the toys sold in the world are made in China, where there are more than 10,500 toy factories in operation.[3] These factories typically have contracts with large Western toy companies such as Mattel and Hasbro, and they form a complex web of supply chains, with contractors in turn subcontracting production of components— and often of entire products—to other companies.

In 2007, toy consumption in the United States totaled nearly $23 billion, while domestic toy production in the same year was only $3.2 billion. And in that year, the United States exported about $2 billion of toys. These figures indicate that domestic production meets only 5 percent of the demand for toys in the U.S. market, while imports meet the rest. Imports from China meet nearly 85 percent of the U.S. domestic demand for toys. With the increase in toy imports, employment in the U.S. domestic toy industry shows a corresponding decline, from 42,300 workers in 1993 to 17,200 workers in 2007.[4]

There are many players in the U.S. toy industry. Although the latest figures are not available, an estimated 880 companies operated in the dolls, toys, and games manufacturing industry in the United States in 2002 (10 percent less than the 1,019 companies that operated in 1997). However, approximately 70 percent of these companies employ fewer than 20 persons.[5] A few key players dominate the industry: Mattel, Hasbro, RC2, JAAKS Pacific, Marvel, and Lego. For a long time, Mattel has been the world's primary toy company, showcasing leading brands such as American Girl, Barbie, Fisher-Price, Hot Wheels and Matchbox. After Mattel comes Hasbro, which is a leading producer of board games and boys' toys. Hasbro markets Milton Bradley, Parker Brothers, Playschool, and Wizards of the Coast, among others. The combined sales of Mattel and Hasbro totaled about $9.5 billion in the year 2009; together these two companies accounted for nearly 12 percent of total global toy sales. The sales of many other major players were under $1 billion.

Although U.S. toy companies have shifted their production overseas, the U.S. toy industry is still the world leader because the domestic operations of toy companies include high value-added activities, such as product design, engineering, strategic marketing, corporate functions, and research and development. As a result, "the majority of toys destined for the American market are designed in the United States."[6] In addition to developing designs at their headquarters, toy companies also buy concepts from independent toy inventors and designers. Further, toy companies license characters from entertainment and educational companies, such as Disney, Warner Brothers, Viacom (Nickelodeon), Origin Products, and Sesame Workshop. For example, Mattel bought exclusive access to characters such as Winnie the Pooh, Disney Princesses, Cars, Dora the Explorer, Go-Diego-Go, SpongeBob SquarePants, Polly Pocket, Batman, Superman, and Elmo. In short, toy design takes place largely in the headquarters of toy companies, most of which are American companies. The toys are then made in China and other developing countries. Very few Western toy companies maintain their own manufacturing facilities in China or other developing countries; thus the majority of toys made in China are produced through contract manufacturing.

The process of outsourcing is not easy, as Mattel's strict multistep process illustrates. The design teams create a bid package containing the new product's blueprint and engineering specifications, and often a physical model of the toy as well. After selecting a contract manufacturer, Mattel establishes the contractor's production infrastructure. At this point, Mattel assumes responsibility for the cost of tooling. The contractor then produces 50 units as "first shots" to verify whether any tool modifications are required. This is followed by one or more "engineering pilots," depending on the toy's complexity, and then by the "final engineering pilot." At this point, a "production pilot" of 1,000 units is run using the entire assembly line to produce the product. Finally, the "production start" phase begins only when the new toy has met design compliance.[7] In other words, while contract manufacturers in China actually make many of the toys, the brand-owning companies monitor and control the production, at least in the initial stages.

Despite its processes, Mattel has faced several recalls over the years. Therefore, it is not surprising that smaller companies, which may not have similar systems in place, also face recalls—things can go wrong at any stage of the manufacturing process. Such incidents might be the result of opportunism, as reflected in substitution of low-priced material for high-priced material, or inadequate crafting. As a result, the final products may not be exactly the same as what was contracted for. It is also possible that the design of the toy could have been flawed to begin with. If suppliers in China (and other developing countries) are acting opportunistically by compromising materials, components, or processes, then more and more recalls would occur due to manufacturing flaws. If, however, the initial designs of the products were inadequate, manufacturing is not the source of the problem.

In short, the United States is a top consumer of toys, but the toys sold there are made in China. However, the toys made in China are mostly designed in the headquarters of toy companies, the majority located in the United States. As a result, the global toy supply chains neatly separate design, manufacturing, and consumption in different parts of the world.

Design Flaws, Manufacturing Flaws, and Other Causes of Hazards

According to the CPSC, a "defect could be the result of a manufacturing or production error; or it could result from the design of, or the materials used in, the product. A defect could also occur in a product's contents, construction, finish, packaging, warnings, and/or instructions."[8] Simply put, a recall could arise as a result of a design or manufacturing flaw or the manner in which consumers have used the product.

Design flaws stem from structural product features that are present in every single one of the units manufactured.[9] Such flaws are inherent to the product design itself; therefore, the hazard exists regardless of where the product is manufactured. For example, Mattel recalled its Batman Batmobile cars in 2004. These cars had tail wings of hard plastic with pointed ends, which posed a potential puncture and laceration hazard. Following 14 reports of injuries, Mattel provided replacement wings that did not have pointed ends and easily snapped onto the toy.[10] Although these toy cars were made in China, it is inconceivable that this problem could have been related in any way to the manufacturing process. The pointed wings were aesthetic aspects of the toys and were likely integral to the product design itself.

At times, a given product design may not meet the regulations that specifically govern its industry. For example, hair dryers are required to have electric shock protection devices (ground fault circuit interrupters or "GFCIs") so that electrocution does not occur if the dryer falls into water while in use. This requirement followed a number of hair dryer-related electrocution deaths in the 1980s.[11] Hair dryers without this integral feature may be recalled, as when electric handheld hair dryers were recalled on three occasions in 2009 because they lacked the immersion protection feature.[12]

Sometimes, products may be produced and sold in spite of the fact that they have been banned by law. For example, in 2008, Modell's

Sporting Goods recalled about 130 diving sticks made in Taiwan. These diving sticks were intended for underwater activities, such as retrieval games and swimming instruction. The CPSC had banned them, however, back in 2001 because they presented an impalement risk to children jumping into pools.[13] In such cases, depending on the severity of the issue, the CPSC may impose a penalty on companies selling defective or dangerous products, in addition to recalling them. Chapter 8 deals with this issue at length.

Design flaws do not necessarily mean that the product was ill-conceived or is inherently flawed. More often than not, designers may fail to anticipate the kinds of problems that are encountered in real life. For example, Maclaren—known for making quality strollers—had to recall about one million strollers in November 2009. The recalled strollers, in and of themselves, were safe. Rather, the problem stemmed from the realities of their day-to-day use. Little children were placing their fingers into the hinge mechanism when the strollers were being folded and unfolded, which caused fingertip amputations, a problem that was likely not envisioned by Maclaren and other companies during the design process. The recall of these strollers was necessary because the usage problem presented a significant risk of injury, one that could be prevented with some simple design modifications. Hence, as part of the recall, Maclaren issued fabric covers that fit over the hinge, preventing children from reaching into the mechanism.[14] Interestingly, this issue affected other strollers as well; other manufacturers, such as Graco, Britax, and Regal Lager, announced a similar fix.[15]

While product design flaws may not be foreseen at the time of design, manufacturing flaws occur when a company deviates from design specifications. Generally, manufacturing flaws involve the use of hazardous materials and incomplete or incorrect assembly. For example, Pokémon recalled plush toys in 2005 because they contained tips of sewing needles.[16] Obviously, the toy's design did not cause this danger. In all likelihood, the needles and pins found their way into the stuffing because of lack of adequate care during manufacturing. Several examples of the use of unacceptable materials, including things like excess lead in surface paint or cadmium in jewelry, can be found in the recall notices.

Manufacturing flaws may also arise due to incomplete or incorrect assembly or production. For example, Fisher-Price recalled Learning Pots & Pans in 2008 because one of the toys in the set, a blue pan, did not have the necessary screws on some units. As a result, the plastic cover came loose and released small balls, which presented a choking hazard to young children. As part of the recall, Fisher-Price asked consumers to examine the bottom of the blue pan to ensure that it contained six screws. If the units did not have all six screws installed, consumers were asked to contact the company to receive a replacement.[17]

In addition to design flaws and manufacturing flaws, products may also pose a hazard due to the nature of their use or lack of adequate instructions and warnings. Often, products may be used in a manner the designers did not intend or by those for whom the product was not designed. For example, it is very common for younger children to use products designed for older children, becoming injured in the process. On the face of it, the consumer is at fault. However, regulators, courts, and consumers themselves take a different view. If a product is accessible to children and can therefore pose a danger to them, these groups expect the company that makes the product to eliminate that danger. For example, Playskool recalled nearly 255,000 tool bench toys because a pair of 3-inch plastic nails that came with the tool bench had resulted in the deaths of two small children, both under two years of age. These children suffocated when the nails became lodged in their throats. The nails were not small parts and the toy tool bench was intended for use by children three years and older. Nevertheless, these toys were recalled simply because they were accessible to younger children and hence posed serious danger to them.[18]

Other times, incorrect instructions may accompany products. For example, Toys"R"Us recalled four thousand Baskets of Bubbles craft sets because the instructions accompanying the sets mistakenly directed children to microwave the soap disks for ten minutes rather than ten seconds. In one case, when the disks were microwaved for ten minutes, the soap and its container melted; in another case, flames occurred.[19] For obvious reasons, these products were recalled.

A further complication stems from the fact that, increasingly, a number of products are assembled by the consumer at home, leaving scope for incorrect assembly and, thus, creating potential hazards. Therefore, product recalls can also occur due to incorrect installation and assembly by consumers. For example, in May 2006, Aqua-Leisure Industries recalled inflatable pools because some consumers had assembled the support clips for the plastic steps upside down, causing the ladder steps to break under a user's weight. This problem was later prevented by color-coding the clips and ensuring that the right and left clips could not fit into the opposite side's locking slots.[20]

On occasion, even a few trained installers have been known to incorrectly assemble products and thereby create a safety hazard. In December 2007, GE recalled 92,000 wall ovens because the installers might have incorrectly attached the door, allowing heat to escape and posing burn or fire hazards. This issue was eventually rectified by redesigning the door hinge so that the door could not be incorrectly installed.[21] Although such cases of incorrect assembly may be few and far between, there is no way of knowing which products have been incorrectly installed or assembled. Therefore, when injuries occur, the involved firms have little choice other than to recall all the units sold and redesign them to eliminate the hazards.

In short, recalls may occur due to flaws in product designs or defects in manufacturing. They may also occur due to inadequate instructions, incorrect assembly, and incorrect usage by non-targeted consumers. There are very few recalls in this latter category, and they can often be avoided by simply refining product designs. For this reason, the analysis in this book focuses primarily on design flaws and manufacturing flaws.

Toy Recalls Due to Design Flaws and Manufacturing Flaws

The recall notices of the CPSC do not clearly indicate whether a given recall is due to a design or manufacturing flaw. However, it is possible to infer whether the flaw was likely part of the original product plan (design flaw) or a deviation from the original plan (manufacturing flaw) that affected certain batches. Such inferences can be made by examining all the descriptive information available in the notices, such as number of units involved, problem descriptions, photographs and sketches, date codes affected (where available), dates on which the product was sold, remedy offered, as well as additional information from the company Web sites that are linked to the CPSC's recall notices.[22]

For this study, the information in the recall notices and the data collected from related sources was used to code the flaw type as one due to design or manufacturing in 558 of the 710 total recalls (79 percent of the cases) issued between 1990 and 2009. In the rest of the cases, the information available was not adequate to infer whether the flaw was design or manufacturing. Further, these cases also included recalls for unintended use and lack of clear instructions. There was no discernible pattern to the recall causes that could not be coded as design or manufacturing.

Figure 5.1 shows that, over the last two decades, a large number of recalls have occurred because of design flaws. From 1990 to 2009, the number of recalls due to design flaws stood at 412, or 58 percent of all recalls. In contrast, the recalls due to manufacturing flaws numbered 146, nearly 21 percent of all recalls issued. However, since 2006, the number of recalls due to manufacturing flaws has been increasing. For the first time, 2007 marked a year in which there were more recalls for manufacturing flaws (43) than for design flaws (25). Since then, manufacturing flaws have remained at nearly the same level as design flaws. Manufacturing flaws were negligible in the 1990s, but have increased several times in the 2000s, particularly since 2006.

The data reveal that design flaws have not decreased over the years; they have, in fact, remained stable. Manufacturing flaws, however, have increased in the recent past. Consequently, the proportion of toy recalls due to design flaws has decreased, while the proportion of toy recalls due to manufacturing flaws has increased. During the 1990s, the proportion of design flaws averaged nearly 75 percent of all recalls, while the proportion of recalls for manufacturing flaws was less than 10 percent. During the 2000s, however, the proportion of recalls for design flaws decreased to about 51 percent on average, while that for manufacturing flaws increased to about 23 percent. In the latest five years (2005–2009), the proportion of recalls due to manufacturing flaws increased to nearly 34 percent on average, while the proportion of recalls due to design flaws stood at 41 percent.

As discussed in chapter 2, recall counts alone may not provide a complete picture because, even with increased recalls, the actual number of units recalled may still be lower. An examination of the

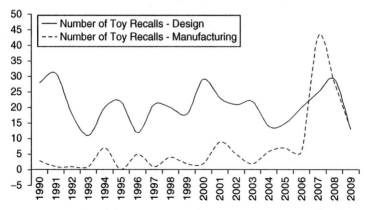

Figure 5.1   Number of toy recalls by flaw type

recalls by the number of units involved reveals that although manufacturing flaw recalls have increased in the recent past, the number
of units involved in each recall was not always large. As a result, the
number of toys recalled due to manufacturing flaws was much smaller
compared to those recalled for design flaws (please see figure 5.2), a
fact that holds true for nearly every year from 1990 to 2009, except
1994 and 2004. In both these years, millions of toys were recalled for
excess lead paint. In 1994, nearly one million crayons imported from
China were recalled,[23] and in 2004, over 150 million toys made in
India were recalled. Barring 1994 and 2004, the proportion of toys
recalled for design flaws remained much higher than the proportion
of toys recalled for manufacturing flaws.

In recent years, then, it is evident that manufacturing flaw recalls
have increased, but also that they have not involved as many toys as
recalls for design flaws. In 2007, manufacturing recalls increased to
43 and involved nearly six million toys. In the same year, design flaws
were responsible for only 25 recalls but involved about 13 million
toys. Hence, in 2007, for example, we see that although manufacturing recalls numbered about 70 percent more than design recalls,
the actual number of units that were recalled due to manufacturing flaws was less than half those recalled due to design flaws. In
2007, the average recall size for a manufacturing flaw was 138,760
units, whereas for design flaws, it was 521,319 units. In 2008 and
2009, the number of recalls for design and manufacturing flaws was
nearly the same, but the number of units recalled for design flaws far
outstripped the number recalled for manufacturing flaws—nearly 15
times more in 2008 and 4 times more in 2009.

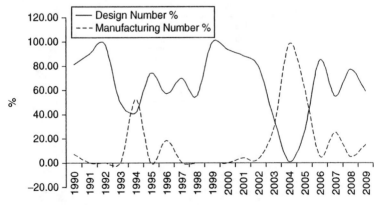

Figure 5.2   Proportion of toys recalled for design and manufacturing flaws

The data presented in figures 5.1 and 5.2 include recalls of all toys, irrespective of where they are made. In order to examine whether the upsurge of Chinese manufacturing has contributed to this trend, we need to study only the recalls of toys made in China. However, as nearly all toys sold in the United States are made in China, these same trends hold for toys made in China as well.

Analysis of Chinese-made toy recalls showed the same pattern of higher design flaw recalls and lower, but recently increasing, manufacturing flaw recalls, as figures 5.1 and 5.2 depict. In addition, the analysis showed that even with their recent increase, the manufacturing flaw recalls involved fewer units, whereas design flaw recalls have involved an increasingly larger number of units. In fact, the average size of a manufacturing flaw recall (of Chinese-made toys) remained nearly the same—about 150,000 units—during the 1990s and the 2000s. In contrast, the average size of a design flaw recall (of Chinese-made toys) increased dramatically during this period, from about 46,000 units in the 1990s to nearly 424,000 units in the 2000s. This increase might reflect the enormity of today's global supply chains, which keep churning out toys before the flaws in them can be detected. Alternatively, it could also be because large toy companies with huge market power are now designing and selling more toys, and thus more toys may be involved in an eventual recall.

The data on Chinese-made toy recalls shows that design flaw recalls have remained stable, but that they have involved greater numbers of units in recent years. This means that in recent years, recalls have affected more consumers because more toys are now involved. The increase in the number of toys recalled for design flaws is indeed a cause for concern. At the same time, it also indicates that the greatest potential for improvements in toy safety exists on the design side.

Even though manufacturing flaw recalls involve fewer actual units, their increasing incidence is also a concern. The rise in manufacturing flaw recalls indicates that manufacturing problems have now become widespread. In order to understand this issue better, a closer look at the issue of manufacturing flaws that reveals the specific kinds of problems that can affect toy safety is necessary.

In short, the majority of toy recalls over the last two decades occurred due to design flaws, but even so, manufacturing flaw recalls have increased in recent years. However, the number of toys recalled due to design flaws has always remained much higher, including in the recent past. This suggests that efforts for improving toy safety are best expended on the design side. Furthermore, manufacturing flaws now seem to affect more and more products, a situation that requires further examination.

Nature of Manufacturing Flaws

Although manufacturing flaws have long caused recalls, the number of such recalls historically has been small. This situation, however, has changed in more recent years. During the 1990s, toys were recalled only 25 times for manufacturing flaws. But in the 2000s, toys were recalled 121 times for manufacturing flaws. In other words, in the latest decade, the number of recalls due to manufacturing flaws was nearly five times more than those in the previous decade. The vast majority of manufacturing flaw recalls are due to excess lead in surface paint.

The use of lead paint on toys provides certain advantages for toy manufacturers. First, lead paint is brighter than non-lead paint. Lead pigments are also highly opaque; thus, a relatively small amount can cover a large area. Further, lead allows the coating to stay tough for a longer period, while at the same time remaining flexible and crack-resistant. In addition, lead adds to the weight of the toys, a trait that is of particular value in jewelry, where weight can connote quality. Finally, lead is cheaper than some of its nontoxic counterparts.[24]

Although lead has advantages for manufacturing, it is also toxic and has been shown to affect health and development. For this reason, the use of lead in paint has been regulated and/or banned in many developed countries. Many developing countries continue to use lead in their paints, either because there is no regulation to govern its use or because the regulations are not enforced. In developed countries, the only potential source of lead exposure is from paint; lead exposure in developing countries can occur due to lead in gasoline, ceramics, mining, batteries, and even in medication and cosmetics.

Since young children tend to put everything in their mouths, lead paint on toys creates a risk that children will ingest lead, which can severely affect their growth and, in extreme cases, cause death. For example, a four-year-old boy in Minnesota died in 2006 after he swallowed a bracelet charm that had been given away with shoes made by Reebok.[25] The recalled bracelets, like many other products recalled for excess lead, were made in China.

For many years, excess lead on surface paint has been a major concern. Between 1990 and 2009, there were 119 toy recalls due to problems with excess lead. Of these, 82 occurred within the last three years of this study period (2007–2009). In short, from 2007 onward, nearly all recalls due to manufacturing flaws were related to the issue of excess lead in the surface paint of the affected toys.

Of the 119 recalls of toys due to concerns over excess lead, 91 of them (about 75 percent) involved toys made in China. This proportion increases to 81 percent if only the latest decade (2000–2009) is considered and becomes 88 percent if only the latest five years (2005–2009) are considered. Table 5.1 shows the number of lead recalls in the last two decades, as well as where each recalled toy was made.

Nearly all toys recalled for excess lead from 1999 to 2009 were made in the developing world, particularly in China. During the entire study period, toys made in China accounted for the highest *number* of recalls for lead in toys. However, by *volume*, toys recalled for lead made in India far outstrip those made in China. This is largely because of the two major recalls in 2004, discussed earlier, that involved toy jewelry. The data show that excess lead in China is a widespread problem that has affected a number of products. In short, made-in-China products account for the vast majority of recalls due to manufacturing flaws, particularly those related to excess lead.

The analysis in this chapter shows that design flaw recalls have historically been higher (than manufacturing flaw recalls), but remained at about the same levels. However, in the recent past, the number

Table 5.1 U.S. toy recalls for excess lead by country of manufacture

Country	1990–1999		2000–2009	
	Number of Recalls	Number of Units	Number of Recalls	Number of Units
China	6	1,066,507	85	9,545,620
China & Vietnam	0	0	1	130
Hong Kong	0	0	4	18,230
India	0	0	5	152,400,630
Indonesia	0	0	1	9,200
Israel	1	10,000	0	0
Japan	0	0	1	300
Korea	0	0	1	75,000
Mexico	2	47,000	1	2,200
Taiwan	1	21,000	2	6,640
Trinidad	0	0	1	2,800
Unknown	3	32,500	3	18,000
United States	1	16,300	0	0
Total	14	1,193,307	105	162,078,750

Source: Author's compilations from the CPSC Data.

of units recalled for design flaws has increased. In contrast, manu-facturing flaw recalls have been lower (than design flaw recalls) for many years, but have also increased in the recent past. The problem of excess lead in surface paint accounts for nearly all manufacturing recalls in the past two decades, the vast majority of which originate in China. Together, these findings indicate that while Chinese manufac-turing practices—particularly the use of excess lead—certainly affect toy safety, the role of inadequate designs created in the corporate headquarters of toy companies should not be overlooked.

Although the majority of designs are made in the headquarters of toy companies, mostly in the United States, it is not completely accu-rate to say that Chinese factories have no role in design flaw recalls. Often, importers and distributors, who do not design toys, simply import toys made in China. Further, as a result of China's dominance in toy manufacturing, a number of retailers have begun to source toys directly from China. These retailers do not design the toys they sell, either. In other words, the toys sold by retailers, distributors, and importers are very likely to be designed and made in China itself. Therefore, in order to better understand the role of Chinese toy fac-tories and importers of Chinese toys in toy safety, it is necessary to examine the recalls by organization type. Hence, the next question is: Are recalls increasing because a large number of retailers and distribu-tors are now importing and selling toys?

Chapter 6

More Players and More Recalls

The global nature of supply chains has changed the mechanics of the toy industry in the United States and elsewhere. A number of companies in China and other emerging economies have begun to specialize in manufacturing. As a result, toy companies that had traditionally focused on toy design, development, and manufacturing have now sharpened their focus to design and development, and have offshored the manufacturing piece. This specialization brings economic advantages because companies can focus on the skills most relevant to that aspect of toy production, but at the same time, such companies may also lose some of their manufacturing skills. In other words, design and manufacturing have now become separated from each other—not just by organizational boundaries, but also by national boundaries— and this separation makes it difficult to ensure an integrated, holistic view of a product since each player is focused on their own individual role.

Further, the growth of manufacturing in China has resulted in a trend of companies that have not traditionally manufactured toys beginning to import toys. These companies do not design toys; they simply source them from China. Such companies fall broadly into the categories of distributors and retailers. The distributors typically import toys made by Chinese companies, which are unbranded or have a very low brand equity. Such distributors are also referred to as importers, but the word *distributors* is preferred since, these days, nearly every company in the toy industry plays the role of an importer. In fact, importing has become an integral piece of the toy business, and it no longer represents a function that distinguishes one company from another.

The toys distributors import are generally not made according to designs and specifications given to contract manufacturers by those distributors. Instead, the distributors see a prototype and make a deal with the overseas manufacturer to import a certain number of units and facilitate sales in the domestic market. Unlike toy manufacturers like Mattel and Hasbro, who traditionally design and make toys, distributors lack the experience and skills related to design and manufacturing. They simply select a toy based on its likely saleability in the target market. This does not mean that the distributors lack the necessary design and manufacturing skills completely, but their skills are considerably inferior to those of the toy manufacturers, who have designed, developed, and produced toys in their own facilities for years.

In addition to the advent of distributors into the toy market, the rise of retailers is also of note. Big retailers like Wal-Mart and Target have become major players in the United States, selling a major portion of the products made by toy companies like Mattel and Hasbro. For example, in 2009, Mattel's three retailers accounted for approximately 40 percent of Mattel's worldwide sales (Wal-Mart at $1.0 billion, Toys"R"Us at $0.7 billion, and Target at $0.5 billion).[1] Considering the fact that these retailers do not operate in several of the international markets in which Mattel sells its toys, the retailers' share of the United States' market (as a percentage of total sales) is quite large. For example, it is estimated that Wal-Mart accounts for about 25 percent of the annual toy sales in the United States,[2] while the top five retailers account for about 60 percent of all toys sold annually in the country.[3] Not surprisingly, these retailers wield considerable influence not only with Mattel but with other toy companies as well. As a result of the big-box retailers' entry into the toy industry, specialty toy retailers like Toys"R"Us have steadily lost market share.[4] Clearly, the specialization formerly attached to toymaking and selling has given way to generalization.

The retailers themselves control the shelf space on which toys are viewed, and more importantly, they have direct contact with parents and children through in-store purchases, coupons, and flyers. For these reasons, retailers have adopted a process of sourcing their toys directly from China. Similar to those purchased by distributors, the toys imported by the retailers are not made according to designs provided by the companies that sell them. Rather, the retailers generally select the toys based on samples. The overall process is the same as that followed by a distributor, as explained earlier, except that a distributor no longer serves as an intermediary and hence does not get paid. This process eliminates the middleman; as a result, the prices of toys can be lower than they would be if a distributor or a domestic manufacturer was involved. Retailers often sell the toys they import under their own brand names. For example, Wal-Mart sells toys under its Kid Connection brand, while Target sells toys under its Play Wonder brand.[5]

In addition to retailers and distributors, other companies, such as food companies, computer companies and financial services companies, often import toys to give away as promotional items to their consumers. For example, Dunkin' Donuts gave away glow sticks with the purchase of donuts in 2007; Gateway offered foam-rubber toy cows with the purchase of computers in 1999; and State Farm handed out stuffed bears between 2005 and 2007. All three of these toys were later recalled.[6] Unlike retailers and distributors, who continuously import toys, these companies do so only sporadically to give away as promotional items, but just like the retailers and distributors, these companies lack the necessary skills and experience to assess the toys they distribute for potential safety issues. In fact, the skill and experience levels of these companies are likely to be even lower than those of retailers and distributors.

Figure 6.1 presents a simplified value chain of toymaking. The major activities of the process can be categorized into design and development, manufacturing, distribution, and sales. As presented, traditional toy manufacturers increasingly focus only on downstream activities such as toy design, development, and manufacturing. Often, these toy manufacturers also outsource toymaking to companies in other parts of the world. They do, however, enjoy full control over design and development and at least partial control over manufacturing even when the toys are made in supplier factories. In contrast, distributors—and occasionally non-toy companies—focus on importing toys made in factories in China and other such countries. Finally, retailers focus on distribution, marketing, and sales.

The diagram in figure 6.1 is not the most accurate or detailed presentation of the value chain of toymaking. For example, it does

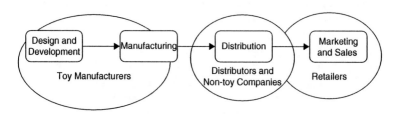

Figure 6.1   Toy value chain and types of organizations

not include direct sales by toy manufacturers over the Internet. Also, some distributors and retailers may exercise more influence than others over the design and manufacturing processes. Barring such exceptions, the diagram is a fair schematic representation of toymaking and of the types of organizations concentrated at each stage of the process.

In short, the global nature of toy-industry supply chains has enabled a number of different kinds of companies to import toys. The major types of organizations that distribute toys are manufacturers, retailers, distributors, and some non-toy companies. Manufacturers have traditionally developed and manufactured toys and, hence, have more experience and skill with respect to their products than the other types of organizations. For this reason, it is important to examine whether recalls are associated with particular types of organizations.

Toy Recalls by Organization Type

The CPSC's recall notices provide information on the name of company that recalled the product. These companies were categorized by searching various data sources to gather information about their business operations.[7] Based on the information collected from these sources, companies were categorized into manufacturers, distributors, and retailers. A *manufacturer* is defined as a toy company that designs its products and then manufactures them internally (even if such manufacturing is done offshore) or outsources the manufacturing to factories in China and other such countries. For example, companies like Mattel and Hasbro are manufacturers because they design and/or manufacture their own products.[8] A *distributor* is as an entity whose primary activities include importing toys and related products from overseas manufacturers and distributing them to retailers in the United States. For example, companies like Jazzware and OKK Trading are distributors. Finally, a *retailer* is a company that is primarily engaged in retail operations and not in toy design or manufacturing, but that has sourced its products from overseas manufacturers. For example, companies like Target and Wal-Mart were coded as retailers.[9]

Using the above categorization of organizations, each recall was coded as being issued by a manufacturer, a distributor, a retailer, or a non-toy company. These recalls were then aggregated annually for each type of organization. It may be noted that non-toy companies do not appear consistently and regularly. A non-toy company that recalls a toy is unlikely to recall another toy for many years, and as a result, these companies typically feature only once in the database. Therefore, any finding related to non-toy companies will be of theoretical interest only, and no managerial implications can be derived. In contrast, manufacturers, distributors, and retailers operate actively within the toy industry and, hence, repeatedly issue recalls. For these reasons, the analysis presented in this section excludes non-toy companies and focuses on manufacturers, distributors, and retailers.

Further, as the operations of distributors and retailers are somewhat similar, their recalls have been combined for comparison with the recalls issued by manufacturers. Compared to both distributors and retailers, manufacturers differ qualitatively in their toy-related skills and experience, while there may not be much difference between the former two entities.

Figure 6.2 shows the trend in recalls issued by manufacturers and retailers/distributors. To facilitate easy interpretation, the chart presents the number of recalls as a proportion of total recalls issued in each year. Recalls issued by retailers and distributors have been increasing in the last decade; the number of recalls issued by manufacturers has also increased, but to a lesser extent. The trend has been a bit volatile in the last five years, but it is worth mentioning that retailers and distributors issued more recalls than manufacturers in three out of the last five years. Also, the number of recalls issued by retailers and distributors has been increasing over the last three years in particular, while the number of recalls issued by manufacturers has been decreasing.

The recalls issued by retailers and distributors rose from 67 in the 1990s to 136 in the 2000s, which is an increase of over 100 percent.

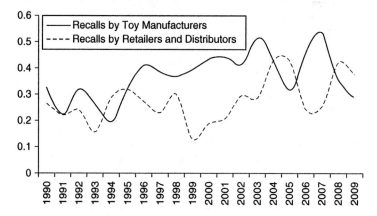

Figure 6.2   Proportion of recalls by organization type

Within this group, retailers issued 75 recalls in the 2000s compared to 31 in the 1990s, an increase of about 140 percent. In contrast, manufacturers issued 85 recalls in the 1990s and 187 recalls in the 2000s, a 120 percent increase. In sum, the increase in recalls was highest for retailers, followed by manufacturers and distributors.

The increase in the number of toys retailers recalled was even higher. During the 1990s, retailers recalled 1.3 million toys; in the 2000s, that number increased to 7 million toys—over five times the number recalled in the previous decade. In contrast, manufacturers recalled 62.5 million toys in the 2000s compared with 38 million in 1990s, an increase of 120 percent. Distributors recalled 4.7 million toys in the 2000s compared with 3.2 million in the 1990s, a 47 percent increase. As with the recalls themselves, the increase in the actual number of toys recalled was much higher for retailers than for manufacturers and distributors. This example illustrates the increasing role of retailers in the toy industry and, therefore, the growing influence their operations have on toy safety.

Figure 6.2 reveals that the recalls by retailers and distributors (as a group) have been increasing in the recent past. However, within this group, retailers issued more recalls and recalled more toys than distributors. This same trait is evident from the top 10 recalling companies, as indicated in table 6.1. For example, Target issued only three recalls in the 1990s, but ten in the 2000s. Other retailers, like Small World Toys and Dollar Tree Stores, have each issued six recalls during the 2000s. International Playthings and OKK Trading (both are distributors) issued seven and six recalls, respectively, in the 2000s.

Although table 6.1 is intended to present only the top 10 recalling companies, for the period from 1990 to 1999, the table lists 13 companies because the last 7 companies issued the same number of recalls. During the entire study period, Fisher-Price was notable for issuing the most recalls. It should be noted that Fisher-Price operates largely in the preschool segment of the market. It is uncommon for companies to focus and operate only in one or two toy market segments, so Fisher-Price is likely an exception. The children in this segment are younger, and their toys are required to meet more stringent criteria. Thus, recalls in this segment are likely to be higher. In other words, the high number of recalls by Fisher-Price must be seen in the context of the market segment in which it operates.

As discussed earlier, the most distinguishing factor between the types of organizations involved in recalls is the extent to which the companies have experience in and control over the design and development of the toys. Toy manufacturers have the most experience related

Table 6.1 Top 10 recalling companies

1990–1999		2000–2009		1990–2009	
Company Name	Number of Recalls	Company Name	Number of Recalls	Company Name	Number of Recalls
Fisher-Price	8	Fisher-Price	18	Fisher-Price	26
Toys"R"Us	5	Target Stores	10	Target Stores	13
Division Sales	5	Mattel	9	Mattel	12
McCrory Corporation	5	Brio AB	8	Playskool Inc	10
Playskool	4	Schylling Associates Inc	8	Brio AB	9
Hasbro	4	International Playthings Inc.	7	Small World Toys	9
Target Stores	3	Playskool Inc	6	Toys"R"Us	9
Mattel	3	Small World Toys	6	Schylling Associates Inc	8
Small World Toys	3	Dollar Tree Stores Inc.	6	Hasbro Inc.	8
Little Tikes	3	OKK Trading Inc.	6	International Playthings Inc.	7
Oriental Trading Company	3			Dollar Tree Stores Inc.	7
Everything's A Dollar	3				
Tara Toy Corporation	3				

Source: Author's compilations from the CPSC Data.

to designing, manufacturing, and selling toys. By virtue of their specialization as toy manufacturers, they are very likely to understand the design of a toy and its probable real-life usage, particularly from a safety perspective, and this capability translates into fewer recalls. In contrast, distributors and retailers may not have as much specialization, experience, or skills to understand how certain features of the toys they source and sell may have hidden hazards. For this reason, retailers and distributors might issue more recalls due to design flaws. Figure 6.3 presents the design flaw recalls by organization type. For easy interpretation, the recalls by each group is presented as a percentage of total design flaw recalls.

Figure 6.3 reveals that, historically, retailers and distributors have issued few recalls for design flaws. Since 2000, however, such recalls have been dramatically increasing. In the last two years of the study period (2008 and 2009), retailers and distributors issued more design flaw recalls than did manufacturers. Although it appears that the design flaw recalls by retailers and distributors decreased in 2006 and 2007, this decrease was simply due to the fact that manufacturers issued more recalls in those years. Manufacturers issued 11 recalls for design flaws in 2006 and 15 in 2007, compared with 7 in 2004 and 6 in 2005. In contrast, the numbers of design-flaw recalls issued by retailers and distributors during the same period remained roughly the same, that is six (2004), seven (2005), seven (2006), and six (2007). In other words, the proportion of recalls issued by retailers and distributors in 2006 and 2007 is lower (than those issued by manufacturers) not because their recalls decreased, but because the recalls by manufacturers increased in those years.

Within the retailers and distributors group, retailers issued more design flaw recalls. The total number of design flaw recalls issued by

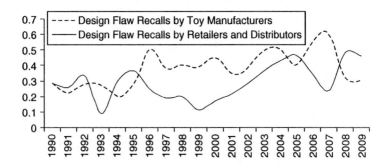

Figure 6.3 Design flaw recalls by organization type

distributors held steady in the 1990s and 2000s, that is, 27 and 29, respectively. However, the number of design flaw recalls by retailers increased from 23 in the 1990s to 41 in the 2000s, a 78 percent increase. In other words, retailers—who lack specific experience in the toy industry—drove the increase in recalls in the 2000s.

Interestingly, although distributors issued about the same number of design flaw recalls in the 1990s and 2000s, the actual number of toys they recalled fell significantly. In the 1990s, distributors recalled about 2.5 million toys, but in the 2000s, they recalled only 1.4 million—less than 60 percent of the number they recalled in the previous decade. This drop indicates that the role of distributors may be decreasing within the toy industry, a trend that is particularly evident in conjunction with the corresponding growth in retailer-issued recalls. During the 1990s, retailers recalled about 1 million toys, but in the 2000s, that number increased to 4.5 million, over four times the number they recalled in the previous decade.

Companies that lack experience designing toys or in the toy industry as a whole may find it particularly challenging to gain an awareness of potential problems, let alone visualize them before selling the products. This point is best illustrated in a November 2008 incident, wherein Target recalled about 365,000 swimming pool dive sticks imported from China.[10] These dive sticks were intended for use in underwater activities, such as retrieval games and swimming instruction. They were rigid, and one side was weighted so that the stick would stand upright on the pool bottom; consequently, they presented an impalement risk to children jumping into pools. The CPSC and toy companies were aware of several impalement incidents that had resulted in injuries to the perineal region of young children. Therefore, in cooperation with 15 manufacturers, the CPSC recalled millions of dive sticks in 1999 and went on to ban the product in 2001.[11] Since the supplier companies, and perhaps the retailers, did not have the requisite toy-industry knowledge (and were likely unaware of the problem), Chinese companies continued to manufacture these dive sticks, and Target continued to import and sell them. Target was not alone: Dollar General and Modell's also sold them, years after their dangers were known within the industry.[12] All sales were eventually discovered and all items were recalled, but this example clearly illustrates how a lack of industry experience can lead to companies unknowingly continuing to sell products that are problematic or even banned.

Some might say that these dive sticks and other toys were likely designed by Chinese toy companies and, thus, the responsibility lies with China. But while the blame may be laid at China's feet, the role of retailers and distributors in selecting, importing, and selling these sticks and other such products should not be ignored. These products were imported only after they were deemed fit for the domestic market by retailers and distributors. In fact, 96 percent of all companies (377 out of 392) that issued the recalls during the study period (1990–2009) were headquartered in the United States, suggesting that U.S. companies play a major role in not only designing and manufacturing toys, but also in importing them. Hence, while the Chinese companies may be faulted for making them in the first place, retailers and distributors who import such products without adequate knowledge and understanding of the domestic market are also to blame.

The uptick observed in recalls issued by retailers and distributors for design flaws was not as evident for the manufacturing flaw recalls. Their numbers moved up and down during the 1990s, but remained higher and appeared to increase in the 2000s. In fact, manufacturing flaw recalls issued by retailers and distributors were higher than those issued by manufacturers in 2003, 2004, 2008, and 2009.

Further examination of the data related to manufacturing flaws showed that, in the recent past, manufacturing flaw recalls by retailers increased more than those by distributors, whose recalls increased more than those of toy manufacturers. During the 1990s, manufacturers recalled a total of 543,263 toys in 8 recalls, compared to 5.2 million toys in 40 recalls in the decade that followed. In other words, the number of toys manufacturers recalled in the 2000s increased nearly two times more than the increase in the number of recalls issued. During the 1990s, distributors recalled a total of 45,400 toys in just 2 recalls, but recalled 2.2 million toys in 23 recalls in the 2000s. That is, the number of toys that distributors recalled in the 2000s increased over four times as fast as the number of recalls they issued. The most astonishing increase was for retailers, who recalled 13,000 toys in 3 recalls in the 1990s, but recalled 1.4 million toys in 17 recalls in the 2000s. In other words, the actual number of toys recalled by retailers increased over 19 times as fast as the number of recalls they announced.

Unlike design flaws, which may have been systemic and which showed a noticeable trend, manufacturing flaws were random and did not show any particular trend. This may be because manufacturing flaws are historically fewer in number, or because manufacturing flaws occur as a result of errors, and there is not likely to be a pattern to such errors. Another possibility is that there may not be any specific factors contributing to manufacturing flaws, which makes it difficult for a trend to appear. However, recalls for excess lead, which represents a very specific and highly dominant manufacturing flaw, showed a clear trend in which lead recalls by retailers and distributors increased in the last two years of the study period, as shown in figure 6.4.

Recalls for excess lead were nearly equally distributed between these two types of organizations (manufacturers and retailers/distributors). Between 1990 and 2009, toy manufacturers issued a total of 37 recalls for excess lead, whereas retailers and distributors issued 39 recalls. The distribution over time, however, is interesting. Before 2007, toy manufacturers issued very few recalls for excess lead. Of the 37 lead recalls by toy manufacturers, only 8 were issued before 2007. In 2007, however lead recalls by manufacturers shot up to 21 and then dropped considerably in 2008 (to 7 recalls), and even further in 2009, when only 1 recall was issued. In other words, lead recalls by manufacturers were generally low throughout the entire study period, with the exception of the 2007 lead crisis.

Retailers and distributors, on the other hand, issued 11 lead recalls before 2007, but these recalls were sporadic in the 1990s. However, since 2001, retailers and distributors have issued lead recalls every year. In fact, in 2007, retailers and distributors issued 11 lead recalls; this increased to 12 in 2008.

The sudden increase across the board in lead recalls in 2007 shows that the lead problem affected all organizations. However, manufacturers seemed to addressed this issue quickly as evidenced by the sharp drop of lead recalls by manufacturers in 2008, followed by a

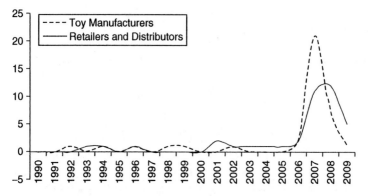

Figure 6.4   Lead recalls by organization type

further drop in 2009. For example, 9 out of the 21 lead recalls issued by toy manufacturers in 2007 involved products sold only in 2007; another 5 involved products sold in 2006. That is, two-thirds of the lead recalls manufacturers issued in 2007 were to recall products that had been recently sold. By 2008, the number of lead recalls by manufacturers had dropped substantially, and the majority of those recalls (five out of seven) were related to recent products. Manufacturers only issued one lead-related recall in 2009, which shows that they appear to have quickly noted the problem, recalled the affected products, and strengthened their manufacturing systems.

Unlike manufacturers, retailers and distributors continued to issue lead recalls in 2008 and 2009. Not only that, but the majority of lead-related recalls by retailers and distributors involved toys sold *after* the 2007 lead crisis. That is, even after the largest crisis in the industry, retailers and distributors continued to import and sell toys with excess lead, toys that eventually had to be recalled. Within this group, distributors were less responsive than retailers, as evidenced by more recalls by distributors in 2008 and 2009 (nine and four, respectively). During the same period, retailers issued fewer recalls: three in 2008 and one in 2009. Even after the crisis, distributors sold and recalled three times more toys than did retailers.

This reveals several interesting insights. First, manufacturers issue more recalls, in general, than do other industry players, which is understandable since they likely sell more toys. Second, retailer-issued recalls have been increasing, and the number of toys recalled by them, both for design and manufacturing flaws, have increased even more significantly. Third, the excess lead problem affected all types of organizations, but manufacturers appear to have corrected the problem first. Retailers followed, while distributors continue to have the highest number of lead-based recalls. These findings suggest that while specific conditions in China may have been the source of lead recalls, the ensuing safety risks were likely exacerbated by lack of organizational systems that could identify and prevent such problems.

Source of Increased Recalls: China or Organizational Systems?

The toy recall crisis of 2007 aptly illustrates the importance of having the necessary organizational systems to prevent and limit recalls. Although the lead crisis affected nearly the entire industry, Hasbro, which is the second largest toy company, did not have a recall for lead. Nor did McDonald's, which distributes a large number of give-away toys with its kids meals.[13] That these companies escaped the lead-recall problem is likely a testament to the strength of their organizational systems, which prevented toys with excess lead from ever reaching the market.

Organizations that have adequate testing and inspection systems can prevent recalls, while those that do not have such systems can at least limit recalls by responding to them promptly, as evidenced by Mattel's actions in 2007. In the summer of 2007, Mattel issued six lead-related recalls, an unprecedented number. The initiative for these recalls did not arise from within the organization, but rather from two outside sources. First, a French direct importer of Mattel's products, Auchan, performed a series of pre-shipment tests with the help of Intertek, an independent laboratory, and found that Mattel's toys contained lead levels that were over the permissible limit. Auchan then presented these results to Mattel. Second, a consumer in the United States used a home test kit and found excessive lead in Mattel's toys. In this case, the customer alerted Mattel directly.

Before the summer of 2007, Mattel required its contract manufacturers to purchase paint from certified suppliers. Alternatively, if they purchased it from noncertified suppliers, the contractors were required to test the paint and the responsibility for doing so was left to them. This system was not foolproof, however, as contractors sometimes failed to test the paint they purchased from the noncertified suppliers. To further complicate matters, Mattel's contractors could subcontract the making of toys; these secondary players did not necessarily follow Mattel's required procedures. Not surprisingly, toys made for Mattel reached the market in spite of the fact that they contained unsafe levels of lead paint.

In response to the recalls, Mattel immediately implemented a three-point check system, which required that only paint from certified suppliers be used and that every single batch of paint at every single facility be tested. The contractors could use only those paints that passed the tests. Also, Mattel tightened controls throughout the production process at its contractor facilities and stepped up its unannounced random inspections. Further, Mattel tested every production run of finished toys to ensure compliance.[14] As a result of these increased inspection systems, Mattel did not face any further lead recalls.

While it is true that the adequate resources of large organizations enable them to act promptly, not every organization with similar resources is able to achieve the same kind of efficient response. For example, RC2 (the manufacturer of Thomas & Friends Wooden

Railway toys) issued lead recalls in 2007 and sent a bonus toy to placate its customers, who were irate about the recalls and dissatisfied with RC2's handling of the recall. In a highly ironic twist, RC2 had to recall about 2,000 additional toys, the very ones that had been sent out to placate the angry customers. This anecdote proves that having resources is certainly a key component of a prompt and effective response to a recall, but resources alone are not sufficient. It is not easy to galvanize an organization on short notice to perform activities that it did not perform earlier. Testing and inspection systems cannot be set up overnight; they have to be developed over a period of time.

It is common to attribute recalls to poor systems in China and, in particular, to poor manufacturing. If that is indeed the case, then we should certainly see an increased number of recalls of Chinese-made toys across organizations. However, as examples like those of Hasbro and McDonald's suggest, poor-quality Chinese manufacturing did not affect all companies. The recall data shows that China did not have a consistent effect on recalls, which leads us to believe that China is not the sole source of recall issues and therefore should not bear the sole blame.

If Chinese manufacturing is truly the major factor in recalls, organizations with less control over Chinese companies and their practices, such as retailers and distributors, should experience more recalls. Also, compared to manufacturers, retailers and distributors should have more recalls because they are less likely to have adequate systems in place and the necessary experience for detecting product flaws. Toy manufacturers, who have both experience and control, should announce fewer recalls. However, no such clear trend was evident in the recalls of Chinese-made toys by organization type.

In fact, the clearest evidence of China's role in recalls is the pattern shown in toy recalls for excess lead (figure 6.4), which clearly demonstrates that lead recalls affected both groups of organizations alike. The problem of lead affected every company, regardless of skill levels, experience in the industry, and apparent control over activities within the value chain. However, the lead problem had a more significant effect on those companies with fewer skills, less experience, and little control over the value chain, a fact borne out in the high and continued occurrences of lead recalls by retailers and distributors.

While it is true that the recalls by retailers and distributors have been increasing, it is also important to place the extent of this problem into perspective. To do this, one needs to examine the number of toys affected. Further analysis of the data revealed that although the number of recalls by retailers and distributors has been increasing and has recently overtaken those issued by manufacturers, the recalls themselves did not involve a large number of toys. As a result, the number of toys recalled by retailers and distributors is far fewer than those recalled by toy manufacturers. For example, manufacturers issued only nine recalls in 2009, but these recalls amounted to 1.75 million units. In contrast, retailers and distributors issued 12 recalls, but these amounted to only 0.36 million units. Compared to manufacturers, retailers and distributors issued nearly 33 percent more recalls, but they recalled 80 percent fewer toys.

The fact that the number of toys recalled by manufacturers is higher although there are fewer actual recalls involved reveals the depth of the problem of defective toys. It also reflects the enormous effect that a lack of adequate organizational systems can have on product quality. If organizations have adequate systems for toy inspection and testing, then product defects can be identified sooner and recalls are, in turn, limited. If, however, organizational systems are weak, then problems are identified later, and more units must be recalled. Of course, the higher number of toys recalled by manufacturers may also be due to the fact that they simply sell more toys. In the absence of sales data from a variety of companies, it is difficult to conclusively suggest that recalls by some types of companies have been increasing. Nevertheless, as the example of Mattel in the lead recalls has shown, prompt response and strengthening of systems could limit recalls and even prevent them in the future.

While the large number of units recalled reveals the depth of the problem, the patterns in figure 6.2 show its breadth, indicating that organizations of all types are issuing recalls. However, as a result of the widespread nature of the problems, organizations with less experience and less control have experienced increased recalls. Figure 6.4 shows how the excess lead problem affected all types of organizations (particularly retailers and distributors), thereby illustrating the importance of *all* organizations having systems in place to identify defective products sooner, recall them more swiftly, and prevent them from happening in the future.

The analysis in this section shows that having industry-specific skills as well as adequate organizational systems is important to prevent and limit recalls. Retailers and distributors, who typically possess less industry experience and exercise less control in the value chain, have been issuing an increasing number of recalls in the recent past relative to manufacturers. The effect of China's manufacturing practices on recalls was evident only in the case of excess lead, which permeated all organizations but was better managed by manufacturers, who typically have more of the necessary experience and also exercise more control. On the other hand, organizations that are less likely to have systems in place—particularly distributors—could not control the problem of lead, even two years after the biggest crisis the toy industry has ever seen.

Of course, problems do exist at the contractors' end, particularly in China. This is evident from the increased recalls in general and the ongoing issues with lead recalls by retailers and distributors. However, poor systems in different types of organizations have exacerbated the problems of poor manufacturing, resulting in more and larger recalls. An increase in recalls, by itself, is not a problem if the recalls are issued swiftly and the defective products recovered fully. Again, organizational systems play an important role in securing this result, and we do not yet know whether organizations have established a standard pattern of identifying defects quickly and responding equally promptly to recall the affected products. Together, these findings bring us to our next question: Are companies issuing the recalls in time?

Chapter 7

Slow to React in a Fast-Paced World

It is easy to see how products can turn hazardous due to ill-conceived designs or erroneous manufacturing. In such cases, recalls are necessary to prevent the product from reaching more customers and to retrieve the unsafe products from the customers. By themselves, recalls are supposed to limit and even prevent safety hazards, but they can miss their mark and create a dangerous situation if they are not announced in a timely manner. Even a few days' delay can mean the difference between few injuries and more injuries, if not deaths, that could have been prevented. As the saying goes, timing is everything, and this certainly holds true for product recalls.

With the rise of the Internet and other communication technologies, it has become easier than ever for companies to quickly identify hazardous products and issue recalls. In addition, through social media, consumers are able to receive information about potentially dangerous products at the click of a mouse or the touch of a keypad. Technology also makes it easier for consumers to contact the CPSC or the companies in question to inform them about potential product hazards. This facility of communication has led to a significant increase in the number of reports the CPSC has received. Given these developments, we should expect that companies would issue recalls more quickly now than in the past and that their response to consumer complaints and CPSC inquiries would be faster as well.

"Time to Recall" over the Years

The first step in the recall process is identifying that a potential hazard exists with a particular product. This information can arise from a number of sources: focus groups organized by companies to understand how consumers are likely to receive a product, actual customers who may have purchased the product and encountered a problem, competitors who may provide a tip about a potential hazard, consumer advocates and testing companies who may review a product and raise concerns, hospitals where affected consumers may have been treated for injuries, investigations by the CPSC, and so on. No matter the source, the first step of a recall lies in recognizing that a potential hazard exists. The company selling the product may take this step and contact the CPSC to take corrective action, or the CPSC itself might identify the problem, in turn asking the company to investigate the issue.

Once the need to investigate an issue has been established, the company and the CPSC jointly discuss and decide on the corrective action needed to eliminate the hazard. If there is a disagreement between the CPSC and the company as to the hazard posed, the need to take corrective action, or the nature of that corrective action, it takes longer to issue a recall. Even after the CPSC and the company agree on a corrective action, the scale of the recall itself and the logistics involved may influence the time it takes to execute the recall; the company must first set up the necessary systems in place.

Overall, the swiftness with which a recall is issued can depend on how quickly the company or the CPSC recognizes the potential hazard, as well as on the cooperation between the two and the company's readiness to conduct a recall. Given the growth in technologies for identifying potential problems and ensuring the flow of information related to the problem, we would expect the recall process to be faster now than ever before. Interestingly, the data appear to provide evidence to the contrary.

The CPSC's recall notices do not indicate when the company informed the CPSC of the potential hazard, or when the CPSC itself recognized it. Also, these recall notices do not include the dates on which the investigations began or the decision was made to issue a recall.[1] They do, however, specify the date the recall was issued and the dates when the recalled product was sold. In some cases, the notices give the exact dates on which the product was sold but, in a vast majority of cases, provide only the month and year. For example, the notice of the recall of Gund Baby Paperboard Books indicates that these books were sold "from January 2009 through March 2010,"[2] and that a recall was announced on April 6, 2010. Therefore, assuming that the products were sold from January 1, 2009, this recall took one year, four months, and six days to come into effect. The entire process of receiving information, recognizing the potential hazard, and coordinating between the CPSC and Gund to launch the recall took 460 days from the approximate first day these books were sold. Since there is no way to know whether the incidents involving these books happened within mere days of purchase or within a year of purchase, it is difficult to determine how swiftly the recall was put in place. Still, in the absence of more precise information, we can examine the date of first sale and the recall date to see whether this time has been increasing or decreasing over the years.

Using the dates of the first sale as a proxy for the date on which the company learned about the problems with its product may not be too far from the truth. For example, after appearing on the market in early 2003, Magnetix toys were recalled on March 31, 2006. The CPSC first became aware of problems concerning magnets in toys when, in March 2000, it launched its own investigation of a magnet-related injury that involved a child who had swallowed more than one magnet from a toy. This investigation revealed that separate magnets could attach to each other from opposite sides of the tissues in a child's intestinal tract. A similar incident occurred in October 2003, and the CPSC was aware of it as well. It is unlikely that the CPSC was developing an awareness of such incidents, but the companies were not. Finally, following a number of incidents and investigations, Magnetix and several other toys with magnets were recalled in 2006 and 2007.[3]

Using the date of first sale and the recall date, the "time to recall" was calculated as the number of days it took for a particular recall to take place. This information was then aggregated for each year to find an average figure for the time to recall, thereby alleviating the effect of the specific factors that may have influenced individual recalls. Recognizing that a few very slow or very fast recalls could skew this average figure, this study controlled for this possibility by also using the median number of days in analysis. The patterns using both mean and median were the same. Therefore, the figures presented in this chapter are mean values.

Figure 7.1 indicates the time to recall has generally decreased in the last two decades. In the 1990s, the average number of days it took for a recall to occur was 806, that is, nearly 27 months. In certain years in the 1990s—for example, in 1991 and 1998—the average time to recall exceeded 1,000 days or nearly three years. In 1993, the average time to recall was the highest, at 1,685 days—a little over four years and eight months. In contrast, the average time to recall during the 2000s was much lower at 566 days or about 19 months. These results show that in the 2000s, the time to recall has become shorter.

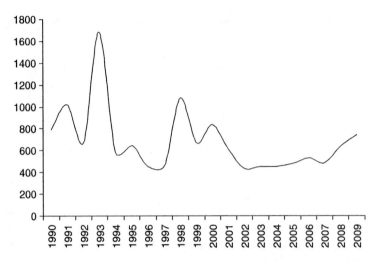

Figure 7.1 Time to recall (in number of days)

Although the time to recall has decreased in the 2000s compared to the 1990s, recent years point to a somewhat disturbing trend. The time to recall appeared to reach an all-time low in 2002 (433 days), but since that time (with the exception of 2007, when there was a drop from the previous year), the time to recall has been gradually increasing. For example, compared to an average toy-recall time of 433 days in 2003, figures for 2009 show an average of 743 days. In other words, a typical recall in 2009 occurred 10 months later than it did in 2003. Likewise, a typical recall in 2009 took 102 days longer than it did in 2008.

This recent increase in time to recall is disconcerting for two reasons. First, during the early years of the CPSC—and even in the early 1990s—it was common to recall toys that had been on the market for several years because many of them had been introduced for sale before certain safety regulations had come into effect. As a result, the average time to recall was, not unexpectedly, higher in the 1990s. Hence, while it may be practical to compare current time-to-recall figures with those of the 1990s, it is not necessarily ideal. Second, given the rise of technology, awareness, and communication, we would expect that in the present day, information flows more rapidly and decisions are made more rapidly too. It is unsurprising, then, that the time to recall is lower in the 2000s than it was in 1990s. But what explains the gradual increase in recent years? To explore this issue, let us examine the excess-lead recalls and the time it took to conduct them.

Time to Recall for Toys with Excess Lead

Given the risks that lead exposure poses, lead should ideally never be used in toys or children's products. In order to discover all products on which lead paint might still be in use, it is crucial to test them and recall them swiftly if they contain excess lead. As presented in table 7.1, nearly one-third of the toy recalls issued for excess lead during the last five years of the study period (2005–2009) involved toys that were recalled during the same year in which they were sold. This is a healthy sign that toys with excess lead are now being swiftly identified and recalled.

One-third of the toy recalls for lead problems in the last five years involved toys that had been sold in the same year as their recall, and another one-third involved toys that had been sold in the year prior to their recall. This means that in nearly two-thirds of cases, the toys sold with excess lead were recalled within the same year or the next. However, 33 percent of the toy recalls were issued at least two years from the time they first appeared on the market. Hence, if these recalls did not take place for at least two years, children were being exposed to lead for a two-year time period or longer. About 11 percent of the recalls involved toys that had been on the market for at least five years. A recall issued after such a long period may not have any useful effect since the damage may already have been done. Once again, public safety requires swift recalls.

Table 7.1 presents a further concern. Despite the toy recall crisis in 2007 and the ensuing special focus on decreasing the lead content in children's toys, the use of lead in toys does not appear to have abated.

Table 7.1   Lead recalls by year of recall and date of first sale

Year of Recall	Number of Lead Recalls	When the Toys Were First Sold				
		Same Year	Previous Year	Two Years Before	Three Years Before	Four Years or More Before
2009	12	1	6	4	0	1
2008	27	7	10	4	3	3
2007	43	19	13	7	1	3
2006	5	3	1			1
2005	5	1		2		2
Toy Recalls (as a %)		34	33	18	4	11

Source: Author's Compilations from the CPSC Data.

In the subsequent two years, there were 30 more recalls of toys for excess lead. Of these, 14 involved toys sold in 2008 or later. In other words, nearly one-third of the lead-related toy recalls in this period (2008–2009) involved toys that were manufactured and sold *after* the 2007 crisis. As discussed in chapter 6, retailers and distributors issued a number of these recalls. On the bright side, the use of lead did decrease following the crisis of 2007, as evidenced by the fact that the majority of lead-related toy recalls in 2008 and 2009 involved toys that had been sold during or before 2007, and only one-quarter involved toys that had been on the market for three years or more.

The lead recall crisis of 2007 was a result of inadequate inspection and monitoring systems, which caused the problem to go undetected for several years. Although the recalls occurred in 2007, the problem had been accumulating for a few years. The average time to recall for toys with excess lead was generally lower than the average time to recall for toys in general. This was particularly true in the 1990s, when the average time to recall was lower than all the other years in this study, except 1993. One particular recall, involving children's puzzles, drove that year's exceptionally high average time to recall toys for lead.[4] This recall involved about 10,000 puzzles made in Israel and imported by U.S. Toy. The red paint in the puzzles contained excess lead; the puzzles had been on the market for nearly 12 years before they were recalled in March 1993.

In the 1990s, the average time to recall for toys with excess lead was generally lower than the average time to recall for all toys. In other words, toys with lead were recalled faster than toys with other defects. By the 2000s, however, the picture changed; the average time to recall for toys with excess lead became about the same as that of all toys, and then it went on to increase. In some years—for example, in 2001 and 2005—the average time to recall for toys with excess lead was nearly double the average time to recall all toys. However, in 2008 and particularly in 2009, the average time to recall for toys with lead was lower than that for any other toys. These figures indicate that toys with excess lead were sold for years before they all were recalled in 2007 and 2008, which caused a sudden spurt in lead-related recalls—and recalls in general.

As companies increased their time to recall, the number of affected toys also increased. Table 7.2 shows that only about half of all toys containing excess lead (49 percent) were recalled within two years of their appearance on the market. While this may seem to be a healthy start toward eliminating the problem, the data in table 7.1 indicated that nearly two-thirds of all toy recalls for lead (67 percent) involved

Table 7.2 Number of toys recalled for excess lead by year of recall and date of first sale

Year of Recall	Number of Units Recalled	Number of Units Recalled by When the Toys Were First Sold				
		Same Year	Previous Year	Two Years Before	Three Years Before	Four Years or More Before
2009	151,866	700	6,230	53,036		91,900
2008	398,054	33,480	62,274	33,800	49,000	219,500
2007	5,966,660	2,161,160	1,751,900	1,778,500	800	274,300
2006	734,300	533,500	20,800			180,000
2005	2,165,240	140		227,100		1,938,000
Total	9,416,120	2,728,980	1,841,204	2,092,436	49,800	2,703,700
Toys Recalled (as a %)		29	20	22	1	29

Source: Author's Compilations from the CPSC Data.

toys that had been on the market for two years or less. In other words, although more toy recalls for excess lead (67 percent) were issued within the first two years of them showing up on the market, the actual number of units involved was far less (only 49 percent). This goes to show that too many toys (about 51 percent) were left on the market for more than two years, exposing children to the dangers of lead for a longer time.

If companies do not issue recalls swiftly, more units of the problematic toy are sold and more children are exposed to the hazard. Table 7.2 provides evidence of the danger that a delayed or slow recall can cause. Although only 11 percent of toy recalls involved toys sold four or more years before their recall date, the affected products constituted 29 percent of all toys recalled. This means that in 29 percent of cases, assuming that parents bought the toys when they were first on the market and that the children had been using them since that time, the affected users were exposed to lead for five or more years. This is not likely to be the case in most instances, but it is certainly possible.

Since swift recalls are important, so are the factors that influence the time to recall, which can include the price of the product in question, the number of units involved, the nature of the hazard, and the type of company.

Factors Influencing Time to Recall

The fastest toy recall on record was conducted by Kellogg in 1991. After giving away 15,576 plush bunnies to consumers in a few grocery stores, Kellogg found that several of the bunnies had broken eyes and noses that posed a choking hazard to young children. These bunnies were given away on March 14 and 15, and the company announced the recall on March 22, a mere eight days after their distribution to the public.[5] As a result of this swift action, the toy did not cause any incidents or injuries. Furthermore, fewer units were involved. Had this recall been delayed, not only would more units have been distributed to the public before the eventual recall, but some injuries would likely have occurred as well.

Table 7.3 presents the 10 fastest recalls of toys during 1990–2009, which range from 8 to 37 days. The time to recall for all toys during 1990–2009 indicates that 153 recalls were issued within six months of the date of the first sale; that is, about 22 percent of toy recalls were issued within six months of the toy's appearance on the market. A total of 333 recalls (or about 47 percent) were issued within a year of them being sold. In contrast to the approximately 47 percent of recalls issued within a year of the first sale, about 24 percent were issued within the second year. However, about 29 percent took more than two years since the date of the first sale of the recalled products. About 7 percent of the recalls were issued more than five years after the toys were first sold. A little over 1 percent of the recalls occurred 10 years after the toys were first sold. Table 7.4 presents the 10 slowest toy recalls from 1990 to 2009.

The slowest recall on record pertains to the recall of WHAM-O backyard water slides. This particular recall was required because the water slides, which were designed for use by children, were also being used by adults and teenagers. Abrupt stops caused permanent spinal cord injury to these individuals, due to their weight and height. In fact, seven adults suffered neck injuries, quadriplegia, or paraplegia, while one teenager suffered a fractured neck. As part of the recall campaign, consumers were advised to read the instructions, which stated that the product was not intended for use by adults. Strictly speaking, this was not a recall; however, the campaign was necessary in order to prevent future injuries. This recall campaign occurred on May 27, 1993; the water slides were sold between 1961 and February 1992. The injuries reported occurred between 1973 and 1991.[6]

In contrast to the recall of the WHAM-O water slides, which simply involved providing consumers with more emphatic instruction about the product's proper use, other delayed recalls have involved modifications to the product or complete withdrawal of the product. In some cases, particularly in the 1990s, the slow recalls involved multiple products or products being recalled by multiple manufacturers. Thus,

Table 7.3 Top 10 fastest toy recalls

Recall Date	Name of Toy	Recalling Company	Date of First Sale	Time to Recall (In Days)	Number of Units Recalled	Average Sale Price	Reason for Recall
Mar 22, 1991	Plush Bunnies	Kellogg Company	Mar 14, 1991	8	15,576	Promotional Item	Several toys had broken eyes and noses(choking hazard)
Oct 29, 1997	Halloween Bounce Balls	Novi Kids	Oct 4, 1997	25	40,000	$2.00	Balls present choking hazard
Oct 29, 1991	Halloween Trumpet sets	Wal-Mart Stores	Oct 1, 1991	28	30,000	$2.00	The trumpet's mouth piece can easily detach (choking hazard)
Mar 10, 1997	Felix the Cat Roller Fun Balls	Determined Productions/ Wendy	Feb 10, 1997	28	800,000	Promotional Item	Small components (choking hazard)
Sep 17, 2002	Chicago Bears Bobble Head Figurines	Bobble Dreams/ McDonald's	Aug 19, 2002	29	100,000	$5.00	Excess lead
Apr 4, 2003	Lamaze Activity Toys	Learning Curve International	Mar 1, 2003	34	3,800	$19.99	Excess lead
Jun 9, 2004	Kiddie Car Cruisers	Far East Brokers and Consultants	May 6, 2004	34	500	$300.00	Unintended acceleration
Aug 6, 2004	Plush Frog Stuffed Animal	Determined Productions/ Wendy	Jul 1, 2004	36	90,000	$5.00	Small components (choking hazard)
May 8, 1992	Doc DeLorean Cars	McDonald's	Apr 1, 1992	37	8,000,000	Promotional Item	Rear wheels of cars can be removed (choking hazard)
Jun 8, 1998	Bubble Beauties Floating Balls	KB Toys	May 1, 1998	38	500	$3.50	Poisonous material inside

Source: Author's Compilations from the CPSC Data.

Table 7.4 Top 10 slowest toy recalls

Recall Date	Name of Toy	Recalling Company	Date of First Sale	Time to Recall (In Days)	Number of Units Recalled	Average Sale Price	Reason for Recall
May 27, 1993	Wham-O backyard water slides	Kransco & Wham-O	Jan 1, 1961	11,834	9,000,000	Not mentioned	Adults using children's product and getting injured
Dec 22, 1998	Toy Basketball Nets	Ohio Art, Little Tikes, Today's Kids and Fisher-Price	Jan 1, 1976	8,391	10,100,000	$30.00	Nets came unhooked or had knots that slid—strangulation hazard if children put their heads into those openings
Aug 13, 2009	Little Tikes™ Workshops Sets and Trucks	Little Tikes Company	Mar 1, 1994	5,644	1,600,000	$62.50	Oversized plastic nails—choking hazard
Oct 22, 1998	Battery-powered cars	Fisher-Price	Jan 1, 1984	5,408	10,000,000	$185.00	Electrical components in the cars can overheat and cause fires
Jul 21, 2000	Baby Jumper Seats and Construction Toys	Fisher-Price	Jan 1, 1987 & Jan 1, 1997	4,950 & 1,297	882,000 267,000	$25.00 $60.00	Spring suspending the jumper seat can break, throwing babies to the ground and strap of the construction toy is long (25-inch), posing a strangulation hazard

Mar 4, 1993	Children's puzzles	U.S. Toy Company	Jan 1, 1980	4,811	10,000	$16.00	Excess lead
Aug 22, 1991	Batting Tee.	General Sportcraft and Foremost	Jan 1, 1980 & Jan 1, 1986	4,251 & 2,059	150,000 70,000	Not mentioned	Injuries occurred when children pulled on the ball or cord and the stake suddenly pulled out of the ground
May 26, 1992	Toy Nursing Bottles	M. Ginsburg & Company	Jan 1, 1982	3,798	144,000	$1.00	Bottle caps separated—choking hazard
Aug 23, 2000	Lift & Lock Swings and Get Up & Go Walkers	Fisher-Price	Jan 1, 1991	3,522 & 1,149	2,500,000 246,000	$19.00 $30.00	Children can maneuver out of the restraints and fall out of swings, and children leaning on the toy can tip them over and fall
Nov 13, 2008	CORAL Swim 'N Score Pool Stix	Modell's Sporting Goods	Aug 1, 1999	3,392	130	$3.00	Children can fall or land on the dive sticks—impalement hazard

Source: Author's Compilations from the CPSC Data.

the problem was somewhat widespread and required action by more than one company. For example, four different companies recalled 10.1 million toy basketball nets in 1998. The recall was necessary because the nets had loops or openings that came unhooked from the rim and/or knots that could slide. If children put their heads into these openings, the net could become tangled around their necks, possibly causing strangulation. As part of the recall, consumers were given new nets that securely attached to the rim and did not have sliding knots.[7] This problem had nothing to do with the way the nets were manufactured but instead arose from a flaw in their design.

Research indicates that design flaws are difficult to identify and thus it takes longer to recall the affected products. It is easier to identify and correct manufacturing flaws because they simply represent deviations from product specifications or from the standards and regulations that govern the product. For this reason, recalls involving manufacturing flaws are generally issued more quickly.[8] This finding is also reflected in the fastest and slowest recalls presented in tables 7.3 and 7.4. Of the fastest 10 recalls, the majority involved either manufacturing flaws or those that could not be easily classified as either design or manufacturing flaws. In contrast, the majority of the slowest 10 recalls resulted from design flaws.

The data presented in tables 7.3 and 7.4 indicate that the price of the product and number of units may not have any bearing on whether a potentially unsafe product is recalled swiftly or slowly. Similarly, the predominance of retailers, importers, and distributors in the top 10 fastest toy recalls and the predominance of toy manufacturers in the top ten slowest toy recalls is not accidental. Research has established that manufacturers take longer to issue a recall compared to importers and distributors, who in turn take longer than retailers.[9]

Manufacturers of toys take longer to issue a recall because information from customers may not always reach the manufacturer. A customer is unlikely to call up a manufacturer and inform them about a product defect. However, if it is a product sold by the retailer, the customer is likely to return it during the next shopping trip. Even though the consumer returned the product, the retailer may not relay specific defect information back to the manufacturer in a manner that would help the manufacturer to take action.

In addition to not being in the best position to receive information from consumers, manufacturers also lack the infrastructure (reverse supply chains) to conduct a recall. For example, systems need to be in place to handle the incoming calls, receive the defective products, dispose of the recalled products, and send new items to consumers.

Since these systems can be difficult and costly to set up, manufacturers may try to resist a recall or may simply need more time to conduct it. As retailers handle millions of products on a daily basis, they are likely to already have in place the necessary infrastructure for a recall, or they can at least set it up quickly.

A manufacturer who recalls a product bears the cost of doing so, unlike a retailer or distributor, who can pass on the costs of a recall to the manufacturer. As a result, retailers and distributors may be more apt to issue a quick recall than are manufacturers, whose profits are affected by recalls. Retailers and distributors are in the best position to receive information about problematic products; they have the systems in place to handle a recall; and they can pass on recall costs to manufacturers. Therefore, retailers are faster to issue a recall than are distributors, who in turn are faster than manufacturers.

To sum up the chapter, the time to recall has generally decreased in the 2000s compared to the 1990s; however, it has shown an increasing trend in the recent past. It is important for the players at every stage in the supply chain to recognize problems as they arise and, in turn, recall the products in earnest. If this does not happen, young children will be exposed to the dangers of defective toys. The recent lead recalls show that the problem had been accumulating for a few years, but was recognized only in 2007. As a result of this delay, a number of toys that were recalled in 2007 had been used for several years. Further, it appears that recalls due to design flaws are issued more slowly than are recalls due to manufacturing flaws. Also, toy manufacturers appear to be slower at issuing recalls than importers and distributors, who in turn are slower than retailers.

Slow or delayed issuance of a recall is, by itself, not problematic if the potential danger is minor or the chances of injury very small. A slow recall is also not problematic if the product has not caused any harm to consumers. In other words, with respect to recall timing, the bottom line is this: it is important to issue recalls before the defective products cause harm to consumers. So, the next chapter examines whether companies are issuing recalls preventively before harm is done to consumers, or reactively, after harm is done.

Chapter 8

More Recalls and Even More Harm

The recent increase in toy recalls can be rationalized in many ways. More toys are sold now than ever before, while at the same time, regulations have become stricter. Thanks to electronic media, society now has a heightened awareness about product safety and, in turn, a correspondingly stronger paranoia. Certainly, children's products must be held to the highest possible safety standards, but companies will still make errors, and slippages may occur anywhere in global supply chains. There is no lack of explanations for the increased number of recalls and no dearth of factors that could result in recalls.

Product defects are not suprising, since they arise largely due to unknown complications or human errors. Of course, such defects could pose hazards, and recalls must therefore aim to eliminate those hazards. Hence, companies must make every effort not only to recall potentially dangerous products swiftly but, ideally, before any harm is done. To that end, it is important for companies to issue recalls in a preventive manner, not just when serious injuries or deaths force the recall upon them.

Preventive and Reactive Recalls

Companies can identify potential defects in products by proactively testing them during the development process itself. For example, tests of reasonable use, abuse, and misuse of a product are conducted on prototypes in simulated conditions. During such tests, potential problems with the final product can be gauged and designs modified to prevent possible hazards. If companies take the prototype testing seriously, they can identify a large number of issues.

It is sometimes the case that companies are unable to identify potential problems before a product is made and sold, and for this reason, tests are often conducted on finished products to reveal potential dangers. During the internal quality checks and inspections, companies may discover product defects that could potentially pose a safety hazard. Alternatively, the CPSC may discover product defects during its ongoing investigations of toys. The CPSC staff may then notify the company and begin the process of investigation, and the company may issue a voluntary recall before any incident or injury occurs. An "incident" is a case in which a given product fails during use, but in spite of this failure, the user does not suffer injury. For example, Bookspan sold Bunny Books in which the seam opened to expose a plastic squeaker toy. A four-month-old infant began to choke on the squeaker, but the parent noticed it and cleared the toy from the infant's throat.[1]

A preventive recall, then, is issued by a company before any incident or injury occurs.[2] It is important to issue recalls in a preventive manner because even an incident indicates a potential harm that was only avoided due to carefulness on the part of users or those around them. Old Navy's 2009 stuffed toy recall is an example of a preventive recall. These toys had two button eyes that could detach and pose a choking hazard to young children, but Old Navy issued a recall before any incident or injury occurred.[3] It is likely that internal tests and inspections by Old Navy helped the company to identify the issue and recall the toys. It is also possible that the CPSC may have identified the potential danger and notified Old Navy.

In contrast to a preventive recall, a reactive recall is one that is issued following incidents, injuries, or deaths. It is likely that companies who issue a reactive recall either lacked internal testing and investigation systems to identify the problem beforehand or overlooked the potential danger. As a result, reactive recalls are issued only after a safety hazard has caused incidents, injuries, or deaths. An example of a reactive recall was Magnetix's recall of magnetic building sets by Rose Art. The magnets in these toys fell out and were swallowed or aspirated by young children. If a child swallowed more than one, the magnets attracted to each other in the intestines and caused intestinal perforation or blockages. The CPSC became aware of 34 incidents involving these toys, including one death and four serious injuries,[4] all of which indicated the need for a recall.

Toy Recalls: Preventive or Reactive?

The CPSC's recall notices include data on incidents, injuries, and deaths. When no incidents, injuries, or deaths preceded the recall, the notice also mentions this fact. This data can be used to examine whether recalls have been preventive or reactive. Using the incident and injury data in a recall notice, all toy recalls were coded as either preventive or reactive. If a recall notice mentioned incidents, injuries, or deaths, then that recall was coded as reactive. Otherwise, the recall was coded as preventive.[5] Note that recalls for excess lead do not contain any data on injuries because the effects of lead exposure are hidden and long term. Therefore, the analysis presented here excludes the recalls for excess lead. It is interesting to note, however, that the patterns presented here remained the same even when excess lead recalls were included in the analysis. This goes to show the robustness of the patterns presented here.

The proportion of reactive recalls in total recalls is presented in figure 8.1, in terms of the number of recalls announced and number of units recalled each year. As shown in figure 8.1, in 1990, only 6 percent of the toy recalls were reactive, that is they were announced only after an incident, injury, or death occurred. Since then, however, this figure has been increasing, reaching a peak of 80 percent in 2009. Although it dropped to about 45 percent in 2005, it then rose again and remains at high levels. In absolute numbers, 20 out of the 25 non-lead-related toy recalls in 2009 were issued only after incidents, injuries, or deaths came to light.

The increase in reactive recalls is even more worrisome when the number of units recalled is considered instead of just the number of recalls. As evident in figure 8.1, the increase in the number of units reactively recalled each year is faster and higher than the increase in reactive recalls. The difference in these two rates of increase may be

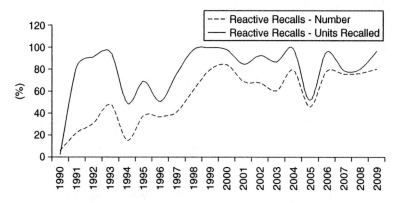

Figure 8.1 Proportion of reactive toy recalls—numbers and units

due to the fact that companies are willing to issue preventive recalls only when the number of toys involved is small. But when the number of toys involved is large, companies may instead decide to take a risk and not issue a recall in order to try and avoid the costs related to the process. In terms of absolute numbers, the decline in the number of toys recalled preventively is even more astonishing. For example, in 2009, the number of toys recalled before any incident, injury, or death occurred was only 82,870 compared to a total of 3.7 million toys recalled overall. That is, only 2 percent of all toys recalled in 2009 were preventive; all the rest were reactive.

To provide a better sense of the types of reactive recalls, tables 8.1 and 8.2 present the top reactive recalls, ranked according to number of deaths or injuries caused by a given product. Table 8.1 shows that only eight recalls issued during 1990–2008 reported deaths in their notices. Of these, Hasbro recalled Team Talkin' Tool Benches after two deaths, while the rest of the toys on the list were recalled following one death apiece. The Team Talkin' Tool Bench was a 20-inch-tall plastic toy tool bench that contained toy versions of a saw, a drill, a vice, a hammer, a screwdriver, and two 3-inch plastic nails. A two-year-old boy was running with one of the toy nails clenched in his teeth when he tripped and fell on his face. The nail shot down his throat and formed an air-tight plug in his trachea. His mother could not pull it out and, hence, intervention was needed. Sadly, time ran out and the little boy died. A similar case had occurred a few months earlier.[6] These nails were not considered to be "small parts," and the tool bench was not marketed as a toy for children under three years of age, which require stricter adherence to small-parts standards. Nevertheless, Hasbro issued the recall and asked consumers to return the two nails in exchange for a $50 certificate toward future Hasbro purchases.[7]

Toys that have caused deaths or that have the potential to cause deaths are obviously dangerous. But toys that cause injuries are also dangerous. Table 8.2 shows that a number of toys were recalled only after injuries occurred. Topping this list was Fisher-Price, who recalled two toys at the same time. Together, these two toys had caused injuries to 170 children. One was a swing from which children were able to maneuver out of. As part of the recall, Fisher-Price provided free repair kits with supplemental waist and crotch restraint belts. Another toy was a walker—a push toy that looked like a car and was intended to be used by children as a support while they were learning to stand and walk. However, when a child leaned forward on the front of the toy car, it could tip, causing the child to fall over. Further, the toy had a protruding windshield wiper that could injure a child when they fell. As part of the recall, Fisher-Price again provided a free repair kit that eliminated the front bar and the windshield wiper.

It may be noted that poor manufacturing did not cause the recalls discussed above; they were caused by integral or planned features of the products. The majority of recalls appearing in tables 8.1 and 8.2 were clearly the result of design flaws, but not because of deviations from product specifications during manufacturing. These problems would have occurred no matter where the products were made. These examples further demonstrate the vast scope for improving product safety through better designs.

On the face of it, the number of deaths and injuries reported with each recall presented in tables 8.1 and 8.2 may seem small, but, for a variety of reasons, recall notices generally underreport the number of incidents and injuries. It is likely that companies and the CPSC may not know the actual number of injuries since some parents may not know where to report such injuries or they may simply choose not to. Even when the reports arrive, companies may not have the proper systems to record them from the very first incidents. It is possible that some companies may ignore the initial reports, attributing them to user errors or even dismissing them as complaints from zealous consumers. In some cases, reports may not come to light because companies often settle claims with parents, holding them to nondisclosure. Finally, companies may simply fail to report the actual numbers or report them late.

As a result of underreporting deaths, injuries, and incidents in the recall notices, it is not possible to know the exact extent of the damage a given recalled product causes. Many cases may never come to light or do so only after in-depth investigation. For example, when Graco recalled its Converta-Cradle R brand swings in 1992, the recall notice indicated that the company had received "reports of four incidents of partial or total suffocation of infants."[8] However, when Boston Globe reporter Kevin Cullen investigated further, he uncovered 12 deaths and about 24 near-death suffocations. These figures were later confirmed, based on the documents filed as part of legal proceedings.[9]

The CPSC and the involved companies jointly announce recalls of consumer products, including toys. It is common for companies to try and underreport any injuries because such information can be used against them in pending or future litigations. Without clearly established evidence that the product was the direct cause of each incident, injury, and death, it is difficult for the company to report

Table 8.1 Reactive toy recalls that involved deaths

Date of Recall	Name of Toy	Recalling Company	Number of Deaths	Number of Injuries	Number of Incidents	Time to Recall (Number of Days)	Number of Units Recalled	Sale Price ($)	Reason for Recall
September 22, 2006	Team Talkin' Tool Bench toys	Playskool/ Hasbro	2	0	2	356	255,000	35.00	Oversized, plastic toy nails became forcefully lodged in children's throats.
April 19, 2007	Magnetix Magnetic Building Sets[a]	Rose Art/Mega Brands	1	28	1,500	1,326	4,000,000	40.00	Magnets can be swallowed, causing intestinal rupture and blockage.
November 6, 1997	Wooden Clown toys	Brio AB	1	0	0	309	79,000	19.00	Small wooden hat caused choking.
April 14, 2004	Ride-on Toy Trucks	Tek Nek Toys	1	0	6	500	70,000	30.00	The screw and nut assembly attaching the steering wheel can come loose, posing a choking and aspiration hazard.
July 21, 2000	Wiggle Waggle Caterpillar Toys	Jakks Pacific	1	2	3	812	1,000,000	13.00	Small balls attached to the toys pose a choking hazard.

December 17, 2009	"Action Team" Toy Dart Gun Set	OKK Trading	1	0	1	1,112	22,000	1.00	The soft, pliable plastic dart can cause choking or aspiration.
March 27, 1991	Decorator Cubes with hinged lids (used to store toys)	Seward Luggage, Trojan Luggage, and Mercury Luggage	1	0	1	1,546	2,200,000	Not mentioned	The falling lid can cause strangulation.
December 22, 1998	Toy Basketball Nets	Ohio Art, Little Tikes, Today's Kids, and Fisher-Price	1	0	20	8,391	10,100,000	30.00	Nets can come unhooked or had knots that slide, a strangulation hazard if children put their heads into those openings.

Note: [a] This information is from the revised notice. The original notice issued on March 31, 2006 contained different figures.

Table 8.2 Top 10 Reactive toy recalls that involved injuries

Date of Recall	Name of Toy	Recalling Company	Number of Injuries	Number of Incidents	Time to Recall (In Days)	Number of Units recalled	Average Sale Price ($)	Reason for Recall
August 23, 2000	Lift 'n Lock Swings and Get Up & Go Walkers	Fisher-Price	170 (38 & 132)	440 (110 & 330)	3,522 & 1,149	2,500,000 246,000	19.00 30.00	Children could easily slip out of the swing or tip over and fall when using walker.
June 27, 2000	Sky Dancers Flying Dolls	Galoob Toys	150	170	2,065	8,900,000	16.50	Dolls can fly rapidly in unpredictable directions, injuring those around.
May 2, 2007	Soft Blocks Tower Toys	Graco	81	137	820	40,000	80.00	Small detachable parts pose a choking hazard.
February 6, 2007	Easy-Bake Oven	Easy-Bake/ Hasbro	77	249	281	985,000	25.00	Children can insert their hands into the oven's opening, causing entrapment and burns
September 7, 2006	Learn-Around Playground Activity Center	LeapFrog Enterprises	54	145	433	186,000	60.00	User's arm could be entrapped in open tube.

October 9, 2008	Nerf™ N-Strike Recon Blasters	Hasbro	46	46	343	330,000	20.00	Toy's plunger can pull the user's skin, causing injuries.
April 29, 1993	Rubber Popper	Quaker Oats	36	36	Promotional item	8,300,000	Promotional item	Eye injury from suction can occur when used in an unintended manner.
June 11, 1998	Bouncing Buggies	Safety 1st	34	700	406	106,000	50.00	Thin protruding parts are easily breakable, posing choking hazard.
July 24, 2007	Sky Rangers Park Flyer	Estes-Cox Corporation	33	45	691	21,000	30.00	Unintended explosions can occur while user is winding up the airplane.
April 19, 2007	Magnetix Magnetic Building Sets	Rose Art/Mega Brands	28	1,500	1,326	4,000,000	40.00	Magnets can be swallowed, causing intestinal rupture and blockage.

them. To further complicate the reporting process, the CPSC cannot provide evidence of a defective product's culpability in each case and is therefore limited in its ability to push the company to report injuries accurately. More importantly, the CPSC tried to initiate a given recall and conduct a rectification campaign in order to prevent future damage rather than to force companies to provide correct information about injuries and deaths. Therefore, underreporting likely continues unabated, as the recent Magnetix recall demonstrates.

The Magnetix building sets recall was issued on March 31, 2006, and reported that the CPSC was "aware of 34 incidents involving small magnets, including one death and four serious injuries."[10] The release also stated that about 3.8 million units were involved. A year later, on April 19, 2007, the CPSC and Mega Brands (who later aquired Rose Art Industries, the supplier of Magnetix) expanded the recall and stated jointly that they were aware of one death, one aspiration, and 27 intestinal injuries. With only one exception, all cases required emergency surgical intervention. The number of incidents was reported to be "at least 1,500," and the number of units involved was revised to be "in excess of four million units."[11]

It is possible for companies to underreport because of constraints related to establishing evidence and the need to issue a mutually agreed-upon recall notice. This situation is likely to change because the Consumer Product Safety Improvement Act (CPSIA) of 2008 put a regulation in place that requires the CPSC to implement a publicly accessible, searchable database of consumer product incident reports. Accordingly, the CPSC plans to build a public database, which "will be a single, central location where consumers can go to report product safety incidents, and to search for prior incidents and recalls on products they own, or may be thinking about buying."[12] This database is expected to be available by March 2011, and it will help to increase the transparency of product safety issues, as every incident reported by every consumer will become publicly available.

It is not correct to say that underreporting by companies always goes unchecked. The CPSC has the power to impose penalties on companies that violate the terms of the Consumer Product Safety Act by underreporting the extent of damage with respect to a given product-related injury. The Act stipulates that companies, "are required to report to CPSC under Section 15 (b) of the Consumer Product Safety Act (CPSA) within 24 hours of obtaining information which reasonably supports the conclusion that a product does not comply with a safety rule issued under the CPSA, or contains a defect which could create a substantial risk of injury to the public or presents an unreasonable risk of serious injury or death."[13] In addition to the CPSA, the CPSC is also empowered by the Federal Hazardous Substances Act (FHSA), Flammable Fabrics Act (FFA), Poison Prevention Packaging Act (PPPA), and Refrigerator Safety Act (RSA). The CPSC can impose civil and criminal penalties on companies that violate the reporting requirements or other provisions of the legislation that the CPSC administers.

Penalties Levied by the CPSC

Although the CPSC is empowered to impose penalties on those who violate statutes, historically, the organization has sought relatively few fines compared to the number of violations it noted each year.[14] This scenario may be changing fast, however, as the recently enacted CPSIA has increased the maximum penalty for each violation of the CPSA, FHSA, or FFA from $8,000 to $100,000. Also, maximum penalty amounts for a related series of violations were increased from $1.8 million to $15 million.[15]

The CPSC also makes available on its Web site the information on any penalties it has levied upon errant companies. For this study, this information was coded to demonstrate any trends in violations committed by companies. The penalties were broadly categorized into two categories: "Failed to Report" and "Others." The former represents violation of CPSC reporting requirements, while the latter broadly deals with selling goods that are prohibited for sale in the United States.

A number of penalties levied by the CPSC have been the result of a given company's failure to report defective products to the CPSC. Two such examples are penalties given to Brinkmann Corporation and L.L. Bean. In 1996, Brinkmann Corporation agreed to pay a $175,000 fine to settle CPSC accusations that the company had knowingly violated reporting requirements for three of its products and that these products were dangerous to consumers. From 1979 to 1993, Brinkmann had sold 1.2 million cooker/fryers, electric smokers, and charcoal water smokers. The company received information during this time of over 20 incidents of burns from use of these products in general and 25 reports of fire from the charcoal water smoker in particular. Several months after it stopped selling these products, in September 1994, Brinkmann voluntarily provided repair kits to owners to fix the problem.[16] In a second case, L.L. Bean received a $750,000 penalty in 2000 for failing to notify the CPSC in a timely manner about problems with the company's child-carrying backpacks. The carriers had a design issue in which children could maneuver their way out of the leg openings at the bottom of the carrier or fall out of the top. The CPSC alleged that the company was aware of at least 39 incidents demonstrating the carrier's danger—including seven injuries involving contusions and lacerations, as well as a case of a concussion and fractured wrist—before it informed the CPSC of any problems.[17] While agreeing to pay the penalty, both these companies denied any wrongdoing. Interestingly, nearly all companies that settle the CPSC's allegations against them deny that they are at fault.

Figure 8.2 shows that the majority of penalties levied by the CPSC are related to companies failing to report problems with their products. The CPSC has levied a total of 315 penalties[18] since 1977; of these, 161 (about 51 percent) were related to failure to report. Between 1990 and 2009, the CPSC levied a total of 263 penalties, of which 137 (about 52 percent) were related to failure to report. In other words, the majority of violations for which the CPSC has imposed penalties were related to failure to report potential product dangers.

The trend toward failure to report product safety issues has been increasing in recent years. For example, failure to report cases represented 41 out of 112 penalties (about 37 percent) the CPSC levied between 1990 and 1999. But, in the following decade (2000–2009), the number of penalties rose to 151, an increase of about 35 percent. But, the cases of failure to report more than doubled, reaching a total of 96—about 64 percent of all penalties. In other words, failure

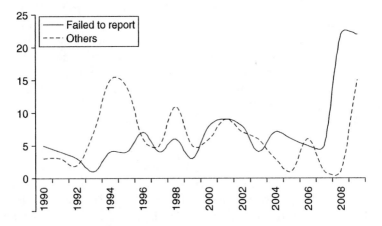

Figure 8.2   Number of penalties by violation type

to report has evolved into a major problem in the area of product safety during the 2000s. If companies do not report or delay reporting potentially harmful issues with their products, then the CPSC cannot take corrective action. In the absence of corrective action, companies continue to sell potentially dangerous products, which are then bought and used by consumers who are unaware of the hidden dangers.

As companies increasingly fail in their obligations to report consumer safety issues to the CPSC, it is not surprising that the number of fines the agency levies have been increasing concurrently. The dollar amount of fines levied for failure to report has also been increasing over recent years. For example, the CPSC imposed a total of $62.6 million in fines on companies for various violations from 1990 to 2009. Of these, $46.6 million (about 74 percent) were due to the companies' failure to report. The amount levied for failure to report increased in the second half of this time period (1990–2009). The CPSC levied a total of $10 million (68 percent of the dollar amount of all penalties) on companies that failed to report during 1990–1999. But these figures increased substantially for the period 2000–2009 as a $36.6 million (about 76 percent of the dollar amount of all penalties) was imposed on companies that failed to report in the next decade.

Failure to report has not only caused the CPSC to impose a growing number of penalties, but also some of the highest penalties ever levied. As table 8.3 shows, 9 of the 12 highest fines are related to failure to report, while the rest are related to importing and selling products with excess lead. Incidentally, of the 315 fines levied, only the 12 presented in table 8.3 involved fines of $1 million or more, thereby raising the question of whether such relatively small fines will in fact deter errant behavior. For several of the companies involved, a $1 million fine is a small price to pay. For example, RC2 Corporation was fined $1.25 million civil penalty in 2009 related to the lead recalls it issued in 2007. In the year before issuing those recalls, RC2's sales were about $519 million and net profits were $34 million. Similarly, Mattel/Fisher-Price was fined $2.3 million for their lead recalls in 2007, while its revenues were $5.65 billion and net profits were about $593 million.

The minor effect these fines might have on companies becomes even clearer when the amount was $100,000 or less. In 177 of 315 cases (56 percent), the fine imposed was $100,000 or less, which could be considered nothing more than a light slap on the wrist; thus, the offending companies did not face a serious penalty for their

Table 8.3 Top 10 fines

Company and Product	Date	Fine Amount ($)	Description of Violation	Incidents	Injuries	Deaths
Graco (Newell Rubermaid) (Toddler Beds & Guardrails)	March 22, 2005	4,000,000	Failure to report; involves 12 million products; most products were sold before the aquisition of Graco by Newell-Rubermaid.	3948	767	6
McDonald's (Big Mac Climber)	June 29, 1999	4,000,000	Failure to report; second violation; first violation settled by agreeing to finance a $5 million children's safety campaign with the CPSC.	Over 400	Over 400	0
Mattel/Fisher-Price (Toys)	June 5, 2009	2,300,000	Importing banned product; company imported toys with lead paint on them.	0	0	0
Cosco/Safety 1st (Dorel) (Cribs/Walkers)	April 4, 2001	1,750,000	Failure to report; companies made design and label changes to violating products, but did not report to CPSC; some products resulted in death and injuries to users.	3,504	303	2
Dynacraft BSC (Bicycles)	November 19, 2004	1,400,000	Failure to report; delayed reporting multiple times (had multiple staggered recalls) of products dangerous to users and surrounding people.	35	35	0
RC2 (Toys)	December 29, 2009	1,250,000	Importing banned product; violated federal lead paint ban; 1.75 million toys recalled.	0	0	0

Company (Product)	Date	Penalty	Description			
Hamilton Beach/Proctor-Silex (Cooking utensils)	March 30, 2005	1,200,000	Failure to report; third violation; involves toasters, juicers, and slow cookers, which all caused injuries to users but were delayed in their reporting to the CPSC by several months.	2,289	6	0
Fisher-Price (Toys)	June 7, 2001	1,100,000	Failure to report; first penalty; company knew their "Power Wheels" vehicles had a defect for years, but only reported after the CPSC contacted them.	116	9	0
Mega Brands America (Magnetic Toys)	April 14, 2009	1,100,000	Failure to report;	1,500	25	1
Brunswick (Bicycle Forks)	September 23, 2003	1,000,000	Failure to report; company recalled several times with increasing injuries each time.	900	1	0
General Electric (Dishwashers)	August 8, 2002	1,000,000	Failure to report; involves faulty wiring in dishwashers that resulted in fires; company knew of 111 cases before they reported information to the CPSC.	111	0	0
Reebok International Ltd. (Jewelry)	March 18, 2008	1,000,000	Importing banned product; Reebok imported chains, which they distributed for free to purchasers of their athletic products.	1	0	1

violations. With the recent revisions to the regulations, however, this situation is expected to change in the near future.

Recently, the CPSC ruled that in determining future penalties, it will consider: "(1) the nature, circumstances, extent and gravity of the violation, including the nature of the product defect or the substance; (2) the appropriateness of the penalty in relation to the size of the business or of the person charged, including how to mitigate undue adverse economic impacts on small businesses; and (3) other factors as appropriate. These factors are in addition to the factors already required to be considered: the severity of the risk of injury; the occurrence or absence of injury; and the number of defective products or the amount of substance distributed."[19] With these clear rulings, future fines are likely to have more of a deterrent effect.

Although cases related to failure to report are increasing and constitute the majority of violations, in the recent past, we have seen increases in other kinds of violations as well. For example, as presented in figures 8.2 and 8.3, the number of violations categorized as "Other" increased from 3 in 1999 to 15 in 2009, and the involved companies were dealt a combined penalty of $5.4 million in 2009 in contrast to $67,000 in 1999. Many of the violations for which penalties were imposed in 2009 involved the sale of goods with excess lead, and most of the involved products were recalled in 2007 and 2008. The importation of banned products is another violation that has received a significant number of penalties. Specifically, this refers to the importation

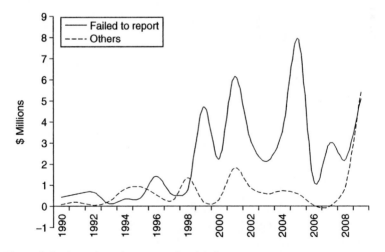

Figure 8.3 Annual penalty amounts by violation

and distribution of products that the CPSC has deemed unsafe for consumption or use in the United States, as explained in sections 17 and 19 of the Consumer Product Safety Act. Companies importing products for sale in the United States must comply with all CPSC statutes and must also record the entry of such products. In 2005, U.S.-based Winco Fireworks was fined $600,000 for importing fireworks that were banned under U.S. law. Winco had previously signed an agreement mandating that all fireworks the company imported would be tested for compliance to U.S. fireworks rules. The CPSC alleged that, after signing this agreement, this company continued to sell imported fireworks that violated the U.S. fireworks law.[20]

In some cases, the CPSC imposed penalties on companies that *exported* products that had been recalled or were found to have violated U.S. consumer product safety standards. CPSC regulation 16 C.F.R. Part 1019 requires that if a company knows the products they are exporting violate a CPSC rule, they must provide 30 days' notice to the CPSC informing it of the product being exported, along with information on the specific violation, the destination of the product, the amount of product being exported, and so on. Following this, unless the CPSC exercises its discretion to prevent the export, companies are free to export recalled products or those that violate a U.S. safety standard. There have been only two penalties levied for violations of the rules governing exporting a banned product. In September 1994, Great Lakes Products paid a $10,000 fine for illegally exporting a chemical called volatile alkyl nitrite.[21] Although the chemical was a legal sexual stimulant in many nations, its use was illegal in the United States, and therefore the CPSC needed to be informed of its exportation. Also in 1994, Walgreen Company paid $50,000 to settle allegations that it exported its Toy Center Musical Phone to China without informing the CPSC.[22] In the United States, the toy phones were recalled due to small parts and were thus banned substances under the FHSA.

Other cases for which the CPSC levied fines relate to the intentional sale of products that violate regulations. An example of this was the case of a Cotton Cloud futon, which Cotton Cloud continued to sell, despite notification of the product's lack of compliance to FFA standards. This violated CPSC regulation, resulting in the allegation that Cotton Cloud had purposely sold illegal products. The company was fined $10,000 in 1995.[23] In a second example, in April 2001, Federated Department Stores (the parent company of Macy's and Bloomingdale's) was fined $850,000 for knowingly selling children's sleepwear that was made of flammable material. FFA regulation states that flammable material must not be used for sleepwear, although it is not illegal for underwear or playwear. The CPSC alleged that retail employees knew and admitted that the violating products were, in fact, sleepwear.[24]

In some cases, penalties have been related to violations of the Poison Prevention Packaging Act (PPPA). For example, Blue Coral-Slick 50 was fined $150,000 in 2003 for failing to label one million bottles and pouches of Rain-X Super Glass Cleaner Concentrate, Rain-X Washer Fluid Additive, and Rain-X Plus Washer Fluid Concentrate that did not have child-resistant closures.[25]

In a rare incident, an employee lied to the CPSC, an act that resulted in a fine and a jail term. In April 2001, the operator of National Marketing, a Memphis, Tennessee, distributor of cigarette lighters, was sentenced to two years in jail for lying to a CPSC investigator regarding the removal of child-resistant mechanisms on lighters. The company itself received a $250,000 fine for this violation.[26]

In conclusion, this chapter reveals that reactive recalls have increased over the years; that is, more and more recalls are issued only after the respective products have caused injuries to users. Also, companies often fail to report—knowingly or unknowingly—to the CPSC about the dangers posed by products they have sold. These companies may quietly redesign the products to eliminate the hazard, or they may simply ignore the reports of harm caused to users. As a result, the CPSC has imposed penalties on a number of companies. Until recently, in comparison to the actual number of violations, these fines were too small and too few to be effective. Recent changes to the related legislation will likely increase such penalties, which should serve as a heightened deterrent for the offending companies.

When companies become aware of problems with their products, they are required to inform the CPSC immediately and also take swift corrective action in order to prevent further harm to consumers. However, an equally important factor in preventing and limiting harm is to effectively recover the sold goods from the hands of the consumers. The remedy companies offer to consumers, such as replacement of product, repair of the product, or refund of purchase price, will influence the consumers' response. Therefore, one might wonder whether companies are making serious efforts to recover dangerous products. The next chapter discusses this aspect of the recall process, examining the patterns that emerge based on the remedy offered to consumers of recalled products.

Chapter 9

Increasing Recalls, Decreasing Remedies

Identifying problems with a product, assessing the need for a recall, and swiftly issuing that recall before much harm is done to consumers—these are only the first steps in a recall process. The most important step, in fact, is not issuing the recall itself, but effectively recovering the flawed products from the hands of consumers. In spite of the importance of this step, research studies and industry insider accounts reveal that consumers never actually return many recalled products.[1]

On average, only about 37 percent of recalled products are returned. The return rates are particularly low for low-priced products, at around 14 percent.[2] The return rates for toys hover around 23 percent. This may be because toys are low-priced items, or because they have a short lifespan for use, that is, the child may have outgrown the toy by the time the recall is announced. Other factors such as the level of potential risk and the chance of injury can also influence the returns. Further, if consumers have used the product successfully for a long time, they are less likely to return it. In short, it is very difficult to motivate consumers to return recalled products.

The first step in ensuring returns is to make consumers aware of the issue through effective communication. Other factors that influence returns come into play only after consumers are aware of the dangers associated with the products in their hands and recognize the need to take corrective action. When the cost of a recalled product is low, consumers may not make the necessary effort to return the product and receive a replacement. It is likely that consumers may simply throw away the products instead of returning them. If the items are thrown away, the potential for them to cause harm is certainly eliminated. However, if the items are neither discarded nor returned, they will likely find their way to other consumers in other households through informal channels, such as garage sales, charitable donations, and even Internet sales. For these reasons, the danger a problematic product poses is not truly eliminated until that product has been returned, repaired or discarded.

In addition to effective communication, there are three other factors that are likely to increase return rates, making the recall more effective: issuing a recall swiftly so that goods are returned before consumers get used to them, providing an incentive that is sufficient to motivate consumers to return the product, and facilitating the return through a simple procedure so consumers will find it easy to participate and will not ignore the recall request. As the analysis related to the time to recall has already shown, even though the time to recall has decreased in the 2000s compared to the 1990s, the more recent years have seen an increase. This trend is not favorable to the effective recovery of recalled products. Therefore, facilitating returns by providing an appropriate incentive becomes even more critical. This chapter examines the patterns in incentives offered to consumers of recalled products to see whether the remedy offered is likely to encourage returns of products or not.

Remedy Patterns in Toy Recalls

When a company recalls any consumer product, it provides the consumer with a remedy to eliminate the danger posed by the product in question. The remedies available are: discarding the product, receiving a repair kit or returning the product for repair, returning the product for replacement/exchange, or returning the product for a refund of the purchase price.

The type of remedy offered depends on a number of factors, such as the availability of a remedy and the cost and feasibility of its administration. For example, when Hasbro recalled Nerf Blasters, it offered consumers a free cylindrical cover to encase the problematic plunger, thereby preventing the plunger from pulling the user's skin.[3] Administering this repair was not only feasible but also a more cost-effective option for the company than refunding the $20 purchase price to each consumer. In contrast, when companies recall toys due to excess lead, it is not possible for them to offer a repair, so they must either refund the purchase price, replace the item with a different toy, or simply ask the consumers to discard the toy. So, for example, Fisher-Price offered a free replacement toy when it recalled 38,000 Go Diego Go boats (sold at $15) for excess lead, whereas Brand Imports asked consumers to simply throw away children's rings (one million units sold at 25 cents each) when it recalled these items for excess lead.[4]

Occasionally, companies may provide additional incentives to consumers for returning the product. For example, when Dunkin' Donuts discovered that the free glow sticks it gave away with the purchase of donuts posed a choking and strangulation hazard, it recalled the products. As part of the recall, the company asked consumers to return the glow sticks and receive a free donut.[5] Similarly, when IKEA recalled stuffed teddy bears that it had sold for about $2 each, it offered a $5 gift card toward another IKEA product.[6] Such cases are fairly rare, however; the most commonly offered remedies involve refunding the purchase price or replacing the recalled toy with an identical or similar toy.

In the case of toys, the remedy most likely to motivate consumers is a refund of the purchase price. Children's preferences change rapidly as they grow, and toys are used for a very short period. As a result, the recalled toy may not still be in use by the time a recall is announced, so a replacement toy is unlikely to be of interest to children and thus their parents. Replacement with a similar toy would likely only be appealing if the recall has been issued swiftly and the children in question have not outgrown that category of toys. Accordingly, toys for which a replacement/exchange is offered are less likely to be returned in a recall situation than toys for which a refund is given.

The CPSC recall notices clearly specify the remedy offered for a recalled product, and this information can be used to understand the patterns in remedies offered over time. Of the 710 toy recalls issued from 1990 to 2009, the remedy was a "refund of the purchase price" in 409 recalls (about 58 percent). Replacement with the same (but unaffected) toy or exchange for a different toy (replacement/exchange) was the remedy in 221 cases (about 31 percent). Other forms of remedy were less prevalent and together accounted for a little over 10 percent of overall recall remedies. For example, companies offered to repair toys about 5 percent of the time and asked consumers to discard toys in about 4 percent of cases. Other remedies, such as offering store credit, constituted about 3 percent of cases.

The most dominant remedy offered was a refund, a healthy trend to observe. However, this remedy has been decreasing over the years, as replacement/exchange of products has been increasing. As presented in figure 9.1, offering to refund the purchase price was the most dominant remedy in 1990s, the solution of choice in 73 percent

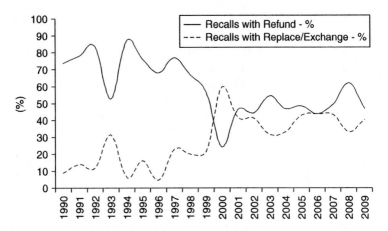

Figure 9.1   Number of recalls by remedy type

of recalls. But in the 2000s, offers to refund the purchase price decreased to an average of 48 percent. Meanwhile, offers to replace/exchange increased to about 41 percent in the 2000s, compared to 15 percent in 1990s. These figures show that the recalling companies are now increasingly offering an inferior remedy than they did in the past, and as a result, it is likely that fewer toys are being returned.

The decreasing trend in offering a refund as a remedy appeared even more dramatic when the remedy type is analyzed by considering the number of units recalled, instead of simply considering the number of recalls. To facilitate this approach, the number of toys recalled each year were aggregated by remedy type. Figure 9.2 shows that the number of units for which refund was offered as a remedy has been considerably lower in recent years.

During the 1990s, companies offered a refund for 29 percent of the toys recalled, but offered the same for only 8 percent of the toys recalled in the 2000s. During the same period, offers of replacement/exchange increased from 22 percent in the 1990s to 26 percent in the 2000s. The decrease in offers to refund the purchase price and the concomitant increase in offers to replace or exchange is particularly evident in the latest five years of the study period. From 2005 to 2009, companies offered replacement/exchange for 75 percent of the total toys recalled, whereas they offered refund of purchase price for only 17 percent of the toys recalled. In absolute numbers, a total of 53.2 million toys were recalled between 2005 and 2009. Of these, a replacement/exchange toy was offered for 39.7 million units, while refund was offered for only 9 million units.

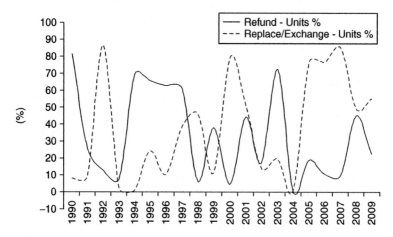

Figure 9.2 Toys recalled by remedy type

In figure 9.2, the percentage of recalled toys for which either refund or replacement/exchange was offered appears to be very low in 1993 and 2004. This is because the remedy for a large number of recalled toys in those two years was, in fact, a request that they be discarded. In particular, Quaker Oats asked consumers to discard 8.3 million units of a promotional toy (Popper) it had given away inside cereal packages in 1993.[7] In 2004, several importers recalled about 151 million pieces of toy jewelry and children's rings whose price ranged from 25 to 75 cents. Users were asked to simply discard the flawed items since it was not feasible to administer any other remedy for such inexpensive toys.[8] Similarly, State Farm recalled about 800,000 stuffed bear toys in 2009 that it had given away in a promotion. These toys had plastic eyes that came off, posing a choking hazard to young children. As part of the recall, consumers were simply asked to discard the bears.[9]

The decrease in refunds compared to the increase in replacements/exchanges is starker when considering the number of units recalled each year instead of the number of recalls. This finding is likely due to the fact that companies may find it economically prudent to offer a refund when relatively few units are involved. When many units are involved, it would be feasible for a firm to rectify the defect in the overall design and then offer an unaffected replacement toy or a similar toy in exchange. As discussed in chapter 2, although the number of toy recalls announced has increased dramatically, the actual number of toys recalled has not increased substantially in the recent past. Therefore, it appears that the decrease in refund offers is reasonably strong evidence of a shifting preference of toy companies when recalling products.

From a company's perspective, it is often economically prudent to offer a replacement/exchange in a recall situation. Consider the case of a company that has to recall a million toys that were sold at $10 each. If the company chooses to offer a refund, then, in addition to the refund cost of $10 million, the company must also incur the costs of receiving the flawed toys and mailing the refund. If the cost of mailing refunds and receiving toys from consumers is estimated to be an additional $10 million, this recall will cost the company $20 million. If, however, the company offers a replacement/exchange toy that cost the company $5 to make, the recall costs would be $15 million. In other words, when companies offer a replacement/exchange, they retain a portion of the profits they accrued through the original sale despite incurring the costs of the recall. When they offer a refund of purchase price, they forego all previous profits, in addition to incurring the administration costs of the recall.

The type of remedy also depends on the nature of the problem. For lead recalls, as an example, the only two options pragmatically available for a reasonably priced product are refund or replacement. For obvious reasons, other options, such as repair, are not feasible for lead recalls. The fact that several companies have preferred to replace defective toys instead of providing a refund is yet another indication that companies are presently offering lesser remedies than they have in the past.

This recent trend toward offering an inferior remedy has several broader implications for recall effectiveness, particularly if it reflects an attitude of companies to provide the minimum in the case of a recall. If companies are providing lesser remedies than in the past, it cannot be expected that they will try harder to recover their defective products. Besides providing an appropriate remedy, effectively recovering recalled products involves spending considerable resources on communicating the recall, setting up systems to handle inquiries from consumers and other stakeholders, and establishing logistics to receive the recalled products. It seems logical to assume that companies whose attitude is "let's offer the minimum remedy" would not be willing to incur the expense of recovering the recalled products.

In sum, it appears that companies are now providing inferior remedies to consumers of recalled products than they have in the past, and the remedy now offered may not be sufficient to motivate consumers to return the recalled products. As a result, fewer products may be returned and companies may be incurring fewer costs of administering a recall, which again benefits the companies but does not necessarily help the consumer.

The analysis in this chapter shows that perhaps companies are now less willing to make efforts to recover their recalled products. The discussion in chapter 7 showed that companies have become slow to recall in the recent past, while chapter 8 demonstrated that companies adopt reactive recalling strategies more often than preventive recall strategies. Together, these findings show that companies have now become less responsive than in the past, an attitude reflected by failing to report defects, recalling only after harm is done to consumers, recalling slowly, and offering less remedy.

It is somewhat understandable that companies have become less responsive to recalls. They may consider the harm to be very minor and improbable, particularly in relationship to the number of products that may have been sold and perhaps used without any incidents. Also, recalls are expensive and are an effort to undo past actions. Expending resources for that purpose may not be as appealing to firms if they lack resources, and even less appealing when those resources could be spent for a number of new and exciting projects that will likely have much greater future benefits.

In short, while recalls are necessary and companies should conduct them when products turn out to be defective, they are crisis situations and, hence, have little appeal to companies. Therefore, the best course of action for companies is to prevent recalls. It is very likely that preventing recalls might be less costly and certainly easier than handling a recall, efficiently or otherwise. Therefore, it is prudent to ask: What can companies do to prevent recalls? The next chapter examines this issue.

Chapter 10

Managing Recalls: Before and After

Toy recalls have certainly increased in recent years, and not surprisingly, nearly all of them have applied to toys made in China. This situation is a direct result of the Chinese economy opening to trade with the rest of the world, particularly Western nations. Like any fledgling economy, China faces a number of issues, such as lax industry regulations, poor working conditions in factories, burgeoning demand for skills to meet the demands of Western markets, and corruption, to mention only a few. Therefore, discussion of toy recalls (and of product recalls in general) has centered on problems that are endemic to China. However, focusing on issues in China or emerging economies alone can lead to incomplete answers and inadequate solutions.

In order to understand product recalls, it is important to dig below the surface-level issues that are related to problems in China and other emerging economies. A critical examination of the toy recalls data in this book has revealed a number of issues that go beyond Chinese manufacturing problems:

- Toy recalls are increasing, but that scenario in itself should not be a cause for concern because the number of units recalled has not increased.
- Recalls of toys made in China are dramatically increasing, but the driving force behind this increase has been the even more dramatic increase in imports from China.
- The source of the problem may not be cost pressures because recalls are not limited to low-priced products; they cut across the price spectrum. In fact, in recent years, recalls occurred more frequently for high-priced toys than for low-priced ones.

- A vast majority of toys were recalled due to inadequate designs the brand-owning companies provided to Chinese contract manufacturers, not to poor manufacturing by the latter. However, recalls due to manufacturing issues have increased in the last few years, largely driven by recalls of products containing excess lead. The recalls for lead shot up dramatically in 2007 and continued in 2008, but a number of the recalled products were on the market for years before they were recalled, pointing to the likely failure of organizations to deal with the institutional differences between the West and Asia, particularly China.
- Although recalls by manufacturers are at a historic high and are increasing, this increase is not so dramatic compared to the increase in recalls by retailers, who have begun to import directly from factories in China, but lack the necessary experience, skills, or organizational systems to prevent recalls.
- The time it takes to recall hazardous toys has been increasing in the last few years, perhaps due to a lack of organizational systems to identify the problems or a reluctance of companies to issue recalls.
- Toy recalls in the recent past have become more reactive than preventive, perhaps due to slower recalls and a lack of organizational systems. The CPSC has substantially increased the number of fines levied on companies that fail to report the problems with their products in a timely manner.
- While toy recalls are increasing, the time to recall is lengthening, and defective products are proving more hazardous to consumers, the remedy offered to consumers has been decreasing. As a result, there are fewer incentives for consumers to return the defective products.

In short, the analysis in this book reveals that while China may be a factor in increased recalls, lack of organizational systems exacerbate the problem. As a result, recalls have not only increased but also have become less effective at protecting consumers. So the question to be asked is not whether China or companies are at fault. Rather, the question should be how we can improve the safety of toys and consumer products in general by decreasing the need for recalls and increasing the effectiveness of those recalls that do occur. The first step in improving toy safety is the responsibility of the manufacturing or importing companies, while the second must be shared between companies and other stakeholders. This chapter primarily focuses on the first step, suggesting that in order to reduce the kinds of situations that necessitate a recall, companies can do a number of things *before* the toy-production phase, *during* the manufacturing process, and even *after* the products are sold. Together, these actions will not only help prevent recalls, but will also make them more effective when they are issued.

The analysis in this book reveals that design flaws are the primary cause of many toy recalls. Further, problems during manufacturing also can lead to a number of product hazards, with certain safety issues emerging because of incorrect assembly by users or inadequate product instructions. In short, problems can occur at any stage of the toymaking process. Therefore, it is important to ensure that, at each stage of toy value chain, no slippages occur. Figure 10.1 presents some examples of potential missteps in the toy value chain, which are elaborated in the following sections.

Preventing Recalls—Before Products Are Made

Pre-production activities in the toy value chain must ensure that the design handed down to the manufacturing stage is safe, sound, and error-free. Such activities include selecting a toy design, developing a prototype, and testing the prototype. These three processes should focus on developing an exciting product but with a safe design.

Thomas Watson, former CEO and Chairman of IBM, is known for saying that "good design is good business," yet many companies still seem to be giving short shrift to design. Industry insiders indicate that only about 1 percent of American companies pay serious attention to design, and very few companies promote executives with design backgrounds to the upper echelons of the organization.[1] Not surprisingly, product designs made by generalist manufacturing corporations won only 7 IDEA awards in 2007, whereas those made by specialist design firms won 14. In the previous four years (2003–2006), manufacturing corporations won 100 awards, while design firms won 128. We can see that, in the past, companies that specialize in design won about the same number of awards as those companies that design products as only one part of their operations. That the number of awards won by manufacturing companies appears to be decreasing perhaps indicates that these companies are paying less attention to design excellence.[2]

As the vast majority of recalls arise due to inadequate design, it is important that companies focus on designing safe toys. Unfortunately, in their haste to be first-to-market, many companies might fail to conduct due diligence on a product, thereby missing the chance to identify any design-related safety issues. Further,

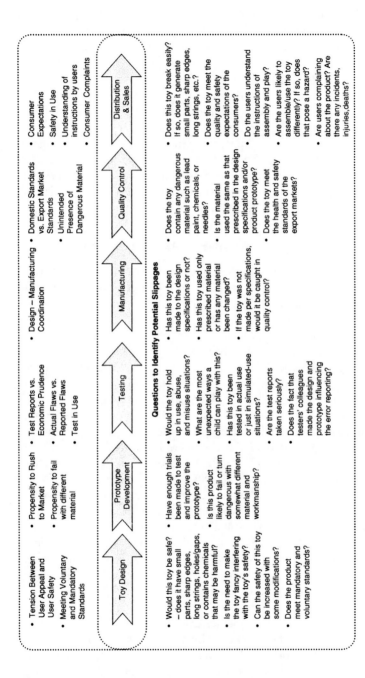

Figure 10.1 Potential slippages in toymaking and addressing them

products are often reviewed and tested for safety within a simulated situation only, and this technique may not be sufficient to identify hazards that could arise during actual use. In order to satisfy the safety expectations of consumers and regulators, product designers must carefully consider every possible way that consumers might use the product.[3] They must specifically focus on whether the product is likely to create hazards during its use. Hence, there are two critical factors for companies to consider when selecting a design: the safety of intended users and the standards and regulations that govern the toy. Inattention to either one can compromise the safety of the toy and lead to recalls.

A consumer-focused design needs to take into account how consumers actually use the final product. This can be accomplished through ethnographic studies of consumers, that is, simply observing consumers as they use the products in their daily lives. Without such understanding, companies might make an otherwise very good product, but with certain problematic features. For example, LeapFrog recalled 186,000 units of playground activity centers because children's arms were getting caught in the plastic tube at center of the toy, resulting in bruises and scratches. LeapFrog announced a recall of these products and provided a repair kit that closed the gaps and prevented children from putting their hands into the tube.[4] Similarly, Regent Sports sold about 190,000 soccer goal nets in which the squares measured five inches on each side. It was found that children were placing their heads into these gaps, either accidentally or intentionally, which posed a risk of head and neck entrapment or even strangulation. Following two such incidents, including the death of a 20-month-old child who was found with his arm and neck tangled in the soccer goal net, the nets were recalled.[5] As part of the recall program, Regent supplied nets in which the distance between knots was reduced to four inches. In these and other similar cases, the design features likely could have been modified and recalls averted if consumer use had been adequately studied and taken into account before the product was manufactured.

In designing products, managers face a major challenge as they must make the product appealing to the user and, at the same time, make it safe to use. At times, it is not possible to strike a good balance between these two goals. Products with sharp features and frills tend to be attractive to consumers, particularly young children; however, they can also be dangerous because the sharp parts pose a laceration hazard and the frills might become detached and pose a choking hazard.

In addition to striking a balance between making a toy fancy and making it safe, toy designers must also ensure that their product meets all the mandatory and voluntary safety standards that govern the product. While this may sound easy to do, it can actually be quite complicated, since there are a number of regulations and standards to be taken into account. Adhering to such safety standards can be particularly challenging for retailers and distributors that do not actually design the product, but rather source the completed item from offshore locations where manufacturers may not have knowledge of the standards that govern the product within the export markets.

Even for the most experienced toy companies, it is difficult to forecast which toy is likely to be successful. Therefore, companies increasingly rely on designs from inventors and entertainment companies. When a company purchases a design from an inventor, the development cycle gets shortened, and the company managers get much less time to reflect on the design than with an in-house design, for which many deliberations may occur before a design is finalized. Also, in the case of characters bought from entertainment companies, it may become challenging to ensure their safe construction while still retaining their original features. For example, Mattel's Batman cars were designed with pointed wings to look like the actual Batmobile. But they had to be recalled as their sharp wings posed a laceration hazard.

Although it is difficult to design a safe product, it is easiest and most efficient to consider safety issues at the design stage. Companies can reduce the possibilities of injury to children and the prospect of a recall by asking explicit questions aimed at ensuring that the toy meets the required standards and its safety has not been compromised in exchange for fancy features. Such questions could include whether the toy meets mandatory and voluntary standards; whether the toy has small parts, sharp edges, long strings, holes/gaps, or contains harmful chemicals; whether specific features that make the toy look authentic interfere with its safety; and whether simple modifications could increase the safety of the toy.

Following the designing phase, the company must develop and test a prototype. In the prototype development stage, the factors that might contribute to missteps relate to the time available for prototype development and the propensity of the toy to fail or become dangerous if alternate materials are used. The toy industry is very competitive and other companies can introduce similar products. In such an environment, there is often a rush to bring ideas to market, especially in the case of toys that are based on movie characters, whose launch must coincide with the movie's release. The rush to get the toy to market may preclude proper testing.

When a prototype is made, developers take a great deal of care and use high-quality materials. In addition, those developing the prototype are very highly skilled technicians. These factors may be absent, however, when the toy is eventually mass produced; for that reason, it is important to consider whether the toy is likely to fail if it is built with somewhat different raw materials or less-expert care. For example, the time between processes in a mass-production system may be forcibly reduced in favor of economic expediency. Consequently, parts of a toy may not be glued adequately or stitched properly. Such eventualities need to be considered at the prototype development stage.

It is not always possible for companies to speculate on the possibility of a toy failing with different materials. For example, faced with several cases of chemical poisoning in children who chewed or swallowed their Bindeez/Aqua Dots toys, Moose Enterprises and its distributors around the world had to issue an immediate recall in November 2007. At that time, Moose Enterprises had no idea why its toys had turned deadly, but investigations eventually revealed that the manufacturer in Shenzhen, China, who made the toys for Moose Enterprises on a regular basis, had substituted one chemical (1,5-pentanediol) with another (1,4-butanediol). Apparently, both these chemicals were widely used in Shenzhen factories, given the large-scale manufacturing that occurs there. The latter chemical (1,4-butanediol) was cheaper but when ingested turned into a compound similar to gamma hydroxy butyrate (GHB). Commonly known as the fantasy or date-rape drug, GHB causes sedation and, in severe cases, coma or death.

Following the development of a prototype, managers should take care to adequately test that item, and such tests should ideally be done in actual-use situations, performed by target users. Too many companies rely on actual people to test product appeal but then use dummies to test the safety features of products such as cribs. The use of dummies is unavoidable in certain cases, such as crash tests for car seats, for example, but in many instances, companies can spot potential dangers by using representative consumers to test the product usage in a more realistic setting.[6] Even if companies are unable to change the product to address such flaws following the tests, they could at least provide clearer usage instructions and warnings.

Testing the toy in actual-use conditions might also help companies to understand whether it could withstand normal use, abuse, and misuse by children. Identifying some of the unusual ways in which children may use the toy or its parts can be very useful for a company. In one example, children who had access to the magnets used in toys did unexpected things, such as putting them in their ears. As a result, medical attention—including surgical intervention—was needed in several cases. These incidents, which were unearthed *after* the production of the subject toys, could have at least been visualized if the products had been tested in actual-use conditions. This would have helped companies to encase the magnets so that they could not become accessible to children, a design feature which toy companies adopted following the large-scale recalls of toys with magnets.

Even more important than testing, however, is the responsibility of senior managers to listen to the concerns of the designers and the testing engineers. Reports from testing engineers are often downplayed or overlooked in favor of economic priorities or in the excitement of taking a new product to market. Graco, for example, produced a cradle in 1989 that did not have a restraint belt to prevent babies from sliding into a corner and suffocating, despite engineers' recommendations to the contrary.[7] As a result, when the product was bought and used by consumers, a number of injuries and several infant deaths occurred. Eventually, Graco recalled all 169,000 units sold.

When designs are created in-house, companies may face another kind of challenge in identifying problems. Testing engineers may not report design problems if doing so could negatively affect their colleagues in the design department. While the testing engineers may not deliberately avoid reporting, they might be somewhat influenced by their relationships or they might downplay potential issues. Therefore, companies need to make sure that testing engineers completely and correctly report all observed flaws to the senior managers.

In short, managers need to pay close attention to the safety features of a toy, particularly ensuring that fancy features do not impinge on the toy's safety. In addition, companies should provide adequate time and resources for prototype development and testing. More importantly, reports from testing engineers should be heeded and incorporated into the final product. These steps will ensure that the manufacturers receive a sound design. In spite of these measures, there may still be evidence of toys that have not been produced as intended or as designed. Given that the manufacturing of toys often takes place halfway around the world, it is equally important to monitor the value chain activities after the toy design is handed over for manufacturing.

Preventing Recalls—As Products Are Made

The steps discussed in the previous section were aimed at creating a sound design, but in order to ensure maximum product safety, it is equally important that the manufacturing is done according to that design. This requires close supervision and quality control during the manufacturing process. As designs are turned into finished toys, companies face three major challenges: first, they must ensure good coordination between design and manufacturing; second, they must ensure that the toys produced meet the standards of the export market; and third, they must eliminate the possibility of unintended materials being used in the final product. Each of these issues is worthy of some discussion here.

In the old days, a firm designed, developed, and manufactured its own products, perhaps all under one roof, which resulted in close coordination between design and manufacturing. However, in the present environment, in which manufacturing takes place in a country halfway around the world by a different company, it is not easy to ensure that the product is manufactured according to design specifications and in the exact manner the designers envisaged. Although designers may develop a product, those who are engaged in its manufacturing actually spend more time with it and are more likely to notice potential problems with the final version. If there is no coordination between the design and manufacturing activities, those involved in manufacturing may simply ignore any problems they spot and let production roll. This scenario is especially likely if the manufacturers have no stake in the overall product or in the brand of the product.

In order to achieve close coordination between the design and manufacturing parts of the value chain, companies must have specific systems and processes in place to ensure that the production process adheres strictly to the design specifications. These systems should provide a feedback loop between manufacturing and quality control and the corporate headquarters that are responsible for the design and overall safety of products. The spate of recalls due to paint with excess lead and other dangerous chemicals highlights these difficulties and points to the complexity of managing such lengthy supply chains.

Not only geographic distance, but also the differences in management practices, regulatory standards, inputs used, and cultural norms make it difficult to ensure a strong link between design and manufacturing. As a result, many companies have resorted to the practice of engaging agents who possess specific knowledge of working in the outsourcing country. The job of these agents is to "get the job done" for the brand companies according to the specifications given to them. But this can also result in serious slippages, as in the following example of the Aqua Dots recall.

A company called Moose Enterprises developed Aqua Dots and then outsourced their production to a Chinese manufacturing company. When that company changed the toy's ingredients, Moose Enterprises was unaware of the change. The source of this misstep was likely the company's agent in Hong Kong, Duo Yuan Plastic Production Company, who in turn outsourced the production to Wangqi Product Factory. Apparently, Wangqi had submitted the production formulas and samples to Moose Enterprises' agent, Duo Yuan, before mass production and had received no objection. It is possible that Duo Yuan did not notice the changes because their expertise was in arranging manufacturing and dealing with Chinese manufacturers, rather than in assessing the impact of formula changes. Or perhaps Duo Yuan simply did not bother to inform Moose about the change because the original material (1,5-pentanediol) was three or four times more expensive than the one used (1,4-butanediol), and so, from a cost standpoint, it was favourable to Duo Yuan. If Duo Yuan had informed Moose, the company would have asked Duo Yuan to use the material per design specifications, which would have cut into the profits of Duo Yuan. Notwithstanding the reasons for this failure of communication, it was Moose Enterprises that bore the brunt of the outrage that followed the recall of the Aqua Dots toys.

Companies can avoid crisis situations like the Aqua Dots recall by coordinating closely with their manufacturers, vetting the suppliers of manufacturers, and monitoring the inputs. While this seems quite achievable, industry insiders suggest that very few brand-owning companies actually work closely with manufacturers and suppliers. In fact, a number of companies have outsourced both production and quality testing to the same manufacturers, a practice that can lead to large-scale systemic failures, as the lead recalls have already shown.

For years, various suppliers were using paint with excessive lead in a number of products. This practice went largely undetected, perhaps because Western companies were unaware of how available and frequently used lead is in China and other developing countries. Not surprisingly, before the lead-related issues in toys began to surface, many companies, like Mattel, asked their contract manufacturers to test the final products to ensure that the paint used on toys was lead-free. Obviously, this system is flawed because contract manufacturers may not have the necessary incentives to meet the standards. This system worked "smoothly" for years, but was eventually found to be flawed, as millions of completely untested products made by thousands of suppliers flooded the market.

Considering the great potential for quality breakdowns between the design and manufacturing phases, it is important for firms to set up their own systems of inspection and conduct them more vigorously. Such inspections would likely identify cases such as missing screws, which resulted in a recall of bunk beds made in Brazil by The Land of Nod[8] and toy pans made in China by Fisher-Price.[9] Working closely with the manufacturers and their suppliers can help to avoid systemic problems such as those related to lead paint as well as other recalls that become necessary because the products have not been made according to their design specifications. However, it is very difficult for retailers and importers, who are less likely to have the required infrastructure or knowledge, to put such practices into play.

Despite the financial and human resources required to monitor manufacturing overseas, there is no substitute for knowing the people, the material, and the norms of the place where the products are being made. Such knowledge can often be used to redesign the products and thus avoid future problems. For example, Indian artisans made toys with soft wood; as a result, finer parts, such as beaks of birds or ears of animals, would easily break off and pose a choking hazard for children. When the importers of these toys interacted with the artisans, the artisans nonchalantly mentioned that soft wood breaks easily and that the users should recognize that fact. For their part, the artisans had taken the nature of wood for granted, since their skill was in carving it, not in predicting its uses. The importers redesigned the toys to eliminate the small parts that were prone to breakage.[10] Even the Aqua Dots toys were reintroduced to the market after they had been redesigned to be covered with Bitrex, which is a safe solution with an extremely bitter taste that dissuades children from placing the product in their mouths. The latter example reinforces the importance of taking manufacturing and user habits into account during the designing process.[11]

Between the design and manufacturing stages of a global supply chain, there are numerous opportunities for slippages. Firms can reduce the scope for these mistakes by creating third-party or self-owned monitoring systems and through increased inspections. These systems would help to ensure the integrity of the final product, making it as safe as possible for use. In addition, companies need to know the manufacturing context of their suppliers, which could help them to redesign products in ways that eliminate any existing hazards.

Preventing Recalls—After Products are Made and Sold

The preceding discussion has pinpointed the need to develop a good design and ensure that production is completed according to that design's specifications. An equally important step in consumer product safety is to communicate the instructions related to product assembly and usage. Managers face a number of challenges at this stage of the value chain, including meeting consumer expectations, ensuring safety by providing instructions that users can easily understand, and—more importantly—monitoring post-sale consumer complaints and taking quick preventive action in response. Managers experienced in marketing are most likely to have the appropriate knowledge to handle these activities.

When it comes to preventing recalls, *marketer* might not be the first word that comes to mind. However, if companies want to be proactive about recalls, they need to make optimum use of the customer knowledge held by their marketing personnel. Undoubtedly, a company's marketing staff has the closest contact with and richest knowledge about product users, and about the market itself, and this knowledge can be parlayed into the redesign of products in order to avoid misuse and danger. Also, companies can use marketing as a way to identify product defects before they turn into full-blown crises. Certainly, a recall made before any harm has occurred to consumers is less damaging to the reputation and the bottom line of the recalling company.

Marketers are knowledgeable about the customers who use a given product, and they can tap into that knowledge to evaluate how the products might be used or abused. Also, marketers can assess whether local consumers will use the product in the intended manner. For example, TTK India is a leading manufacturer of pressure cookers and has sold millions of them in India. When TTK's subsidiary, Manttra, imported these Indian-made pressure cookers for sale in the United States, the parent company soon learned of two incidents where hot contents had spilled out and caused minor burn injuries to the users. Manttra discovered that the incident had occurred because the cooker lids were not closed properly. It is common knowledge among Indian consumers, who regularly use pressure cookers, that the contents of the container will spill out if the pressure cooker's lid is not closed properly. However, consumers in the United States were not as familiar with pressure cookers and did not have a similar degree of knowledge. Therefore, Manttra recalled 38,250 cookers and provided the consumers with a new replacement pressure valve that would prevent opening of the lid until the temperature inside the cooker had dropped to a safe level.[12] This feature has since been incorporated into the more recent designs of the cookers in order to make them safer.

It is very common for younger children to use products that are designed for older children. On the face of it, if an injury to a young child occurs during the use of such products, the consumer is at fault. However, if a product is accessible to children and can pose danger to them, the CPSC and consumers would like the company making the product to eliminate that danger. For example, as discussed in chapter 8, Hasbro recalled nearly 255,000 tool bench toys because the two, 3-inch plastic nails supplied with the tool bench resulted in deaths of two small children, both aged less than two years. These children suffocated when the nails became lodged in their throats. The nails were not small parts and the toy tool bench was intended for use by children three years and older. Nevertheless, the toys were recalled because they were accessible to younger children and posed serious danger.[13] As experts on consumer behavior, it is the marketers who have the knowledge to either foresee such usage or to know about such usage because of their close contact with customers.

The importance of close consumer contact is underscored by the research finding that retailers identify problems and recall the products more quickly than those further removed from the customers, such as manufacturers and suppliers.[14] In 2007, Sears issued a warning to consumers, asking them to remove the label on its Craftsman circular saws. The label on the upper blade guard of the saw became partially detached and interfered with the operation of the lower blade guard, exposing the saw's blade and posing a laceration hazard.[15] There were only two reported incidents, but Sears was able to act swiftly to announce a recall because it was close to the end customers.

As discussed in chapter 5, Toys"R"Us recalled four thousand children's craft sets after just two incidents because the instructions accompanying the set asked children to microwave the soap disks for ten minutes, instead of ten seconds.[16] This simple typographical error, which resulted in a fire hazard, points to the importance of clear and accurate instructions for use of a given product. Instructions need to be both accurate and easy to understand.

Product recalls that occur due to incorrect installation or assembly by consumers are quite common. By paying attention to instances of incorrect assembly, instead of ignoring them or blaming the consumers, companies gain an opportunity to design a preventive mechanism, as in the aforementioned example of Aqua-Leisure, who improved the clarity of its assembly instructions by color-coding the snap-on clips for its pool ladder steps.

When consumers are injured while using a product, it is always possible to at least partially attribute the incident to them. Such situations could take the form of incorrect assembly, improper use, use by unintended users, inadequate skill to use the product, or—in the case of children—lack of adequate parental supervision. However, even if the consumer was at fault or likely contributed to the incident, companies still need to carefully study all such incidents. Attention to consumer complaints and reports may reveal a pattern of errors that can in turn be used to design a safer product.

Ultimately, ensuring that consumers correctly assemble and use a given product is just as important as designing a safe product and manufacturing it according to the design. Managers, particularly those involved with marketing, need to pay attention to actual usage of the product in order to visualize potential problems. Further, managers should also track consumer complaints to examine whether there is a pattern of problems that future designs could address and eliminate.

Preventing Recalls through Better Knowledge Management

Companies can prevent product recalls by ensuring that activities across the value chain are performed carefully. These activities primarily include designing a safe product, manufacturing the product according to its design specifications, and communicating the appropriate methods of product usage to consumers. In order to achieve these three goals, managers must mobilize the vast amount of knowledge available within and outside their organization, leveraging it to ensure safe products.

Product quality can be enhanced by integrative knowledge management, which deals with not only the tacit and explicit dimensions of knowledge, but also with its internal-external dimensions.[17] Explicit knowledge can be articulated and recorded in documents, drawings, and databases. In contrast, tacit knowledge cannot be fully articulated, but rather is revealed in actions by individuals in the course of organizational life. The knowledge that resides within a firm's boundaries is internal knowledge, while the opposite—external knowledge—is held by suppliers, customers, competitors, and others.

A vast amount of knowledge is available to managers, and it can be mobilized to ensure product safety and prevent recalls. As presented in figure 10.2, this knowledge ranges from reports of design engineers within the company to shared understandings between the company and its suppliers.

Explicit knowledge available within the company includes reports of design and testing engineers, as well as complaints received from consumers. The case of Graco, who made and sold cribs without a restraining belt—contrary to recommendations by design and testing engineers—serves as an excellent illustration of how failure to leverage internal knowledge can prove disastrous.

	Internal Knowledge	External Knowledge
Explicit Knowledge	• Reports of design engineers • Reports of testing engineers • Complaints received from customers	• CPSC—Database on recalls to check patterns of problems, investigative reports of CPSC, top dangers outlined by CPSC • Reports published by consumer advocacy groups • Research studies published in medical and other healthcare related journals • Research studies by health and safety experts • Standards related to materials used in toys—legislations around the world • Reports and opinions of consumers on blogs (www.consumerist.com)
Tacit Knowledge	• The concept of safety and acceptable risk—whether it is shared commonly across the organization in various functional areas and across geographical boundaries • Intuitive observations by design and testing engineers about product safety • Handling of unforeseen problems, reporting of issues	• Whether the suppliers share the same concept of safety and acceptable risk as the organization • Whether the suppliers use the same material consistently during the product's life cycle; if they change, how does the change affect the product? • Industry norms, culture, and relationships with suppliers—whether suppliers communicate openly and equally with the company • Supply chain practices in China • Guanxi and relationships, how they override documents and stated requirements • Value of spoken word and relationship over written words and contracts

Figure 10.2   Product Safety and Knowledge Types in Toy Industry

In contrast, explicit knowledge that is available from outside the firm ranges from recall notices of the CPSC to standards governing the product and studies published in medical journals. To name one source, the CPSC database of nearly five thousand recalls is a useful source of information that can help companies to understand what kinds of problems result in recalls. Similarly, studies published in medical journals can often provide insights on how the products may be used in unexpected ways, thus injuring consumers. For example, nearly a decade before small powerful magnets were used in toys, cases of children ingesting magnets and requiring surgical attention were reported in Korea.[18] This was soon followed by another case in the United States, as reported in *The New England Journal of Medicine*, wherein a 10-year-old girl had placed a pair of magnetic rings in her nose. These magnets stuck together in her nose and had to be removed through medical intervention.[19] Another paper reported 24 such cases seen at one hospital in the United Kingdom, ranging from instances of children placing magnets in their ears to ingesting them.[20] In earlier chapters, similar examples of children ingesting magnets and in turn requiring surgical intervention were discussed. If companies had used this knowledge, which was already available from the medical community, then the number of injuries and fatalities that preceded the magnetic toy recalls could certainly have been reduced, if not prevented altogether.

Unlike the explicit knowledge that is available in documents and hence, searchable, tacit knowledge is not codifiable. In order to access tacit knowledge, companies must create a culture of openness in which employees can freely share their observations, even if those observations compromise the immediate financial interests of the organization. While it is difficult to access tacit knowledge within an organization, it is even harder to access it outside the organization. When the suppliers are not treated as equal partners or where cultural differences exist, tacit knowledge is extremely difficult to obtain. An example of this problem can be seen in the challenges that companies face in offshoring their manufacturing to Asian countries. It is highly uncommon for Asian partners and employees to express their thoughts openly, due largely to their culture and upbringing that emphasizes respect to authority and low self-concept due to historical reasons, such as colonization. Further, companies in emerging economies operate within a more informal regulatory culture, in which written contracts receive little weight. For example, if a manufacturing company in China is given a contract instructing that only lead-free paint should be used, that company is less likely than its U.S.-based counterpart to pay attention to it. Instead, the Chinese manufacturer would be more likely to expect that if such requirement was supposed to be met, the brand-owning company would closely monitor the situation, since, in Asian countries, more emphasis is placed on interaction and less on the written words in contracts. If companies do not have tacit knowledge that allows them to understand such cultural nuances, they are likely to operate in the same way they do in the Western world, simply relying on a well-drafted contract.

In sum, managers can reduce product recalls by leveraging the vast amount of knowledge available to them, both within and outside their companies. Any knowledge so leveraged can then be used to create better designs, to manufacture goods according to those designs, and to communicate the appropriate use of products to consumers. However, in order to enhance product safety and decrease product recalls, it is important that other stakeholders play their part as well. These stakeholders include regulators, researchers, and, more importantly, consumers themselves. In the next chapter, we discuss the steps that these stakeholders can take to increase product safety and reduce recalls.

Chapter 11

Managing Recalls: Everybody's Business

Since products are typically recalled because they present harm to consumers, the recent increase in product recalls should be a matter of concern for everyone, especially because the injuries and deaths defective products cause are bound to result in untold societal costs. In addition to physical injury, product defects lead to property damage, which can cause severe financial and psychological distress to consumers. Also, administering recalls and managing recall consequences can be very costly to companies, both financially and in terms of reputation. Certainly, company managers play a major role in the crusade to decrease recalls and increase consumer product safety, but there are other stakeholders as well who should be expected to take part in increasing consumer product safety.

The stakeholders in product safety include researchers, consumers, regulators, consumer advocates, lawyers, politicians, and the media. While each has some influence on consumer product safety, researchers, regulators, and consumers in particular have direct opportunities to prevent recalls. In the following sections, we discuss these opportunities.

Recalls and Researchers

Researchers can play a major role in decreasing recalls and increasing consumer safety by studying recalls in order to generate knowledge that other stakeholders can use. Although recalls are not new, very limited research attention has been paid to this important phenomenon. The research that does exist is disparate and spread across multiple functional areas, which limits the ability of research findings to generate an integrated picture of recalls.[1]

Management research on product recalls has typically focused on two main research questions. First, what are the performance consequences of recalls? And second, how can firms manage recalls? In other words, this research has focused more on what happens after a recall, but has not paid attention to what can be done to decrease recalls. Figure 11.1 presents a research agenda for studying product recalls, generating an integrated understanding of why recalls happen, and finding ways to manage recalls in order to decrease harm to consumers as well as learn lessons that will prevent problems in the future.

The limited research that does exist on recalls has generally focused on the automotive industry. This situation, however, appears to be changing, as the increasing food and consumer product recalls have begun to attract some research attention. In addition, a large number of studies have traditionally been set in the United States, but research on the experience in other countries has increased dramatically in the recent past, perhaps in acknowledgment that consumer reactions are bound to vary depending on the institutional environment and consumer expectations, and thus the results of U.S.-based studies may not be generalizable to other countries. While this is a welcome trend, and one that certainly complements the research conducted in the United States, scholars—both in the United States and elsewhere—must study product recalls in order to highlight some key learning points and identify some patterns. This is particularly important because of the increased recalls in the United States over the last few years and the newly heightened global concerns over product safety.[2]

Many studies have examined the economic consequences of recalls, such as declining stock prices and product demand. Some researchers found that recalls decrease the market value of firms,[3] while others found no such evidence.[4] Those studies that did find an erosion in shareholder wealth noted that the effect was temporary and depended on various factors, including the severity of product's harm, the industry context, and the country context.[5] Studies examining the effect of recalls on future demand and price found that a decrease in demand and price does occur, particularly if the damage was severe.[6] Since product recalls seem to have limited economic consequences for firms, some researchers have expressed doubts as to whether economic consequences alone can prevent future recalls.[7]

In contrast to the research that examined the economic consequences of recalls, research examining consumer reactions found that consumers are indeed critical of the companies who recall products

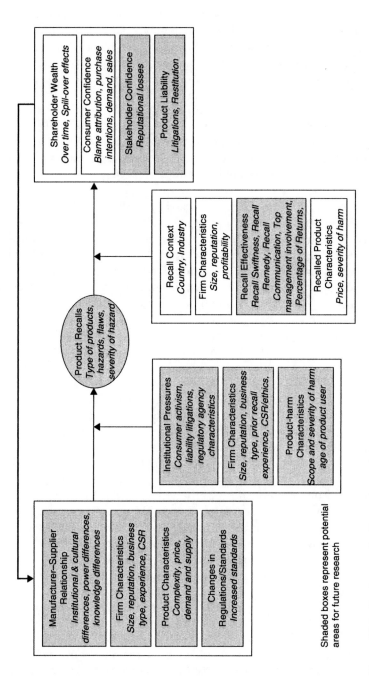

Figure 11.1 Product recalls: Research agenda

Shaded boxes represent potential areas for future research

Manufacturer–Supplier Relationship
Institutional & cultural differences, power differences, knowledge differences

Firm Characteristics
Size, reputation, business type, experience, CSR

Product Characteristics
Complexity, price, demand and supply

Changes in Regulations/Standards
Increased standards

Institutional Pressures
Consumer activism, liability litigations, regulatory agency characteristics

Firm Characteristics
Size, reputation, business type, prior recall experience, CSR/ethics,

Product-harm Characteristics
Scope and severity of harm, age of product user

Product Recalls
Type of products, hazards, flaws, severity of hazard

Recall Context
Country, Industry

Firm Characteristics
Size, reputation, profitability

Recall Effectiveness
Recall Swiftness, Recall Remedy, Recall Communication, Top management involvement, Percentage of Returns,

Recalled Product Characteristics
Price, severity of harm

Shareholder Wealth
Over time, Spill-over effects

Consumer Confidence
Blame attribution, purchase intentions, demand, sales

Stakeholder Confidence
Reputational losses

Product Liability
Litigations, Restitution

but are, in fact, willing to give them the benefit of doubt if the recalling companies are otherwise reputable and manage the recall effectively.[8] While consumers express disappointment when a recall occurs, their response rarely affects the bottom line of the company in the long run. Even so, anecdotal evidence shows that recalls can be costly to companies and may even result in bankruptcies. For example, following Mattel's extensive toy recalls in 2007, consumers filed 22 lawsuits, estimated to have cost the company over $50 million. In another instance, Topps Meat Company was a leading U.S. processor of frozen ground beef for nearly seven decades. However, within a week of recalling over 21 million pounds of ground beef, Topps filed for bankruptcy.[9]

So, barring a few exceptions, research shows that recalls may present temporary losses, but most companies do recover from them. This research is conducted largely from the perspective of companies, not that of consumers or society as a whole. Focusing only on the consequences to companies, using stock price data and consumer reactions, may not reflect the actual damage recalls cause consumers and society. Therefore, it is important that researchers also focus on the non-economic consequences of recalls, including their effect on stakeholder confidence (reflected in reputational losses) and product liability (reflected in the costs of litigations and restitution).

While several studies have outlined the increasing recalls, these studies typically focus on the number of recalls. In order to generate a clearer picture, researchers must broaden their focus and take into account not just the number of recalls but also the number of units recalled, the nature of the hazard posed, the type of defect that has caused the recall, and the extent of the harm posed by the recalled product. Such an examination would provide a nuanced understanding of the recalls phenomenon, as opposed to generating conclusions based only on the number of recall announcements. A more in-depth, richer examination of recalls could provide interesting and useful insights, which would inform further research and public debate.

Research is urgently needed on ways to decrease recalls. It is interesting to note that management research has focused significant attention on the effect of recalls to companies, but it has not studied how those recalls can actually be decreased to prevent those economic losses to companies. In fact, only one study, by Pamela Haunschild and Mooweon Rhee, has examined what companies can learn from recalls. It found that companies issuing voluntary recalls learn to reduce recalls in the future.[10] The findings of this study, which looks at the automotive industry, may not, however, be generalizable to other industries, since recalls of

consumer products are almost always issued "voluntarily in cooperation with the CPSC." Therefore, the learning mechanisms and effects in
these industries may be quite different from each other.

While the inability to learn from past recalls may be a factor in
increasing recalls, a number of other factors may also be contributing to the problem, namely, the institutional differences between the
countries spanned by global supply chains. It is important to research
whether recalls have resulted due to the institutional differences that
exist among the countries where the product is designed, where the
product is made, where the components and raw materials are sourced,
and where the product is consumed. Relationships between manufacturers and suppliers often reflect these institutional differences. In
addition to institutional differences, the differences between manufacturers and suppliers with respect to culture, knowledge, and power
may also increase recalls.

Although recalls may occur for a number of reasons, certain types
of firms may be more prone to creating defective products and, hence,
to issuing recalls. For example, the analysis in chapter 6 shows that
recalls by retailers have increased in the recent years, suggesting that
retailers' inexperience might be a contributing factor. The size of the
company, reputation of the company, orientation toward corporate
social responsibility, and past experience in designing and manufacturing products, could also be examined to see whether they have
any influence on recalls. The analysis in chapter 5 shows that recalls
due to design flaws are historically high and still rising. It is not clear
whether design flaws are in any way related to the type of products
and users involved. For example, nearly half of all consumer products
recalled are toys and children's products. It is likely that products
used by children receive greater scrutiny by regulators and consumers alike. It is also likely that increasingly complex product features
may be contributing to design flaws and other defects. In addition,
as a result of competitive pressures, companies may be rushing their
products to market without due diligence. In short, it is necessary
to examine whether product characteristics are at all associated with
product defects.

It has often been argued that product recalls have increased purely
because of higher standards and expectations. It is not uncommon
to hear refrains such as, "We played with lawn darts that were very
dangerous, but nowadays, even ordinary toys have been recalled."
Companies also say that they are often under pressure to recall products that have been involved only in a few incidents, but are otherwise
safe. Products are now recalled if there is even the slightest chance

that they will cause injury. While this is a good thing, public perceptions need to accommodate this changed scenario. We should know whether product recalls have increased because of poor management or because of today's higher expectations and standards.

Although there can be numerous reasons products might have defects, not all defective products may be recalled. It is likely that institutional pressures, like strong regulations, active consumer advocacy, or rampant litigation cause a number of product recalls. Some point to the lack of recalls in emerging economies and suggest that institutional pressures are in fact a driving force in ensuring that a defective product is recalled. In addition, characteristics of companies, such as size, reputation, and experience may determine whether a defective product will be recalled. Finally, while many products may be defective, it is likely that only those used by children are recalled more often as evidenced by the large number of toy and children product recalls. Therefore, it is necessary to examine what characteristics of institutions, firms, and products moderate the relationship between recalls and their causes.

Research has shown that companies recalling a product need to issue a recall swiftly, communicate it effectively, and manage it efficiently. It is not known whether and to what extent such actions will benefit the companies or reduce the losses. It is therefore important to understand how better management of a recall might affect the relationship between recalls and their economic consequences. Insights from such studies could help companies see the potential benefits of effectively managing recalls and improving their systems and processes.

Research attention is urgently needed to understand the reasons for recalls and how better management can decrease the economic and non-economic consequences of recalls. Studying recalls from the perspective of consumer and societal behavior can demonstrate the real reasons for and consequences of recalls. In addition, research attention is needed to explore the recalls phenomenon in a more nuanced manner, as opposed to getting carried away with the number of recall announcements alone. Research that focuses on these aspects will shed a more useful light on the recalls phenomenon, thereby helping to decrease recalls in the future.

Recalls and Regulators

Next to managers of companies, regulatory officials play the most important role in ensuring consumer product safety. After being dormant for a long time, concern for product safety has awakened in recent years. Consequently, the CPSC has garnered an unprecedented amount of attention and received a major boost in funding and powers. The CPSC is now at crossroads and, in fact, has the potential to change the course of consumer product safety not only in the United States but around the world.

The analysis in this book has revealed several interesting insights that can be used to frame regulatory actions. Chapter 5 showed that the vast majority of toy recalls are due to design flaws. This applies to other industries as well.[11] The CPSC's efforts to improve voluntary standards and mandate product safety mechanisms go a long way toward ensuring that products sold in the United States are based on sound designs. Therefore, the CPSC and other regulators may consider including design analysis as part of the testing that companies must conduct on their finished products. These design analysis requirements can be devised based on the past recalls as well as on knowledge in the fields of human factors, engineering, epidemiology, and other health fields. Considering the vast scope for improvement in consumer product safety (within the area of better designs), incorporating design analysis into testing should be a primary focus of the regulators.[12]

Although a vast majority of recalls are due to design flaws (and these cause more harm to consumers than manufacturing flaws), recent efforts by the CPSC have focused on the safety of imported products. Accordingly, the CPSC has increased port inspections and stepped up its coordination with China in order to ensure product safety. These actions are based on the assumption that the problem lies outside U.S. boundaries. However, as the analysis in this book has shown, the problem may not entirely—or even mostly—lie with China. Instead, the major source of the problem may lie with U.S. companies themselves, including toy companies that design products for manufacture in China and retailers and distributors who import products from China without adequate knowledge of the products they bring in. In other words, while the problems in China and other countries cannot be overlooked, regulators should not ignore the role of domestic companies that import the defective products.

This focus on import safety is appropriate because problems outside the boundaries of the United States affect certain product recalls. These problems are, however, systemic issues, such as the presence of excess lead and other poisonous chemicals in paint. Therefore, efforts should aim to identify and address these issues, rather than merely increase import surveillance in the hope of enhancing consumer product safety. It may also be noted that even the systemic problems in China represent only a small portion of the products recalled. For this reason, it is important to devote optimal resources toward the import-related aspects of product safety. At the same time, it is extremely important that regulators do not focus exclusively on imports, an action that would erroneously devote fewer resources and less effort to decreasing design flaws. As the analysis here and elsewhere shows, the design process affords the most scope for improvement.

The analysis in this book shows that companies may have become less responsive to product safety issues than in the past. This trend is reflected in a general increase in the time to recall, an increase in reactive recalls (those issued only after incidents, injuries and deaths come to light), and a decrease in the quality of the remedy provided to consumers. Recalls are now issued only after products have harmed consumers, and even then, companies may not make a genuine effort to recover the recalled products. This situation reflects a dangerous trend that obviously runs counter to the objective of consumer safety. The recent example of Toyota, who recalled vehicles in the United States only after they were persuaded to do so by the NHTSA (please see appendix A, which outlines a Toyota recall timeline), shows that companies across industries may have become less responsive to consumer safety issues. Therefore, the CPSC and other regulators need to address this and work with the industry to improve the responsiveness of companies. In addition, the recent changes in the CPSIA have enabled the CPSC to impose stricter penalties on erring companies. The CPSC and other regulators could use those powers not only to rein in the erring companies, but also to send a warning to other companies.

One of the issues plaguing consumer product safety is the inaccessiblity of information to consumers. If consumers do not receive information related to a product that has been recalled, they do not return or discard the product and the danger continues to lurk in their homes. Recently, the CPSC made concerted efforts to improve the reach of its recall notices through social media. This push will surely go a long way toward influencing future generations and making them aware of product safety issues in general and recalls issued in particular. The CPSC and other regulators should use social media creatively so that recall-related information reaches the greatest number of consumers in the shortest possible time.

While the lack of *accessible* information is certainly an issue, the lack of *accurate* information related to recalls is an even more serious problem, one that has resulted in some highly charged debates on consumer product safety. This emotional atmosphere generates attention, but it does not help to solve the problems. For example, companies and stakeholders are often quick to blame China for product recalls, and members of the general public, without more information, are just as quick to buy into this mentality.[13] As discussed in chapters 1 and 2, such impressions have generated a bias against imports in general. As we can see from the analysis in this book, and from the developments since the summer of 2007, the issue of product safety is a complex one. Therefore, it is important to maintain a balanced perspective, supported by objective data.

The regulators are in the best position to provide the correct information related to recalls, not only because they have the data at hand, but also because incorrect perceptions can derail consumer product safety, which regulators are supposed to protect. Toward this end, the regulators should engage in more research that can be used to periodically inform the public about recalls, particularly concerning the number of units recalled, the harm caused by the recalled products, the reasons for recalls, and so on. In addition, the CPSC and other regulators should focus on collecting and organizing information on what has lead up to a given product defect. Such in-depth study can help to uncover the exact causes for recalls and may even prevent them in the future. In the absence of correct information, the debate generally gravitates toward frustration over increased recalls and outrage toward China (or some other country where the products may have been made). While this may be accurate in some cases, it is not the truth in general. Therefore, the CPSC and other regulators should provide more nuanced information related to recall trends, as well as correct and complete details on a specific recall at the time of its announcement.

Unfortunately, activities such as analysis, facilitation, and research cannot be easily monitored and tracked in order to assess performance. In contrast, metrics such as the number of recall campaigns or the number of fines levied are easy to count and display as evidence of the regulator's performance. According to this way of thinking, a rise in the number of recalls is evidence that the regulations are working, but in reality, such an approach is somewhat limited in ensuring product safety. To improve product safety, the regulators need to focus on short-term and immediate issues, such as execution of recalls, and on long-term issues, such as research, analysis, and facilitation.

The CPSC and other regulators can increase consumer product safety by analyzing product design processes and providing accurate information to consumers about specific recalls and recall trends.

Such efforts would lead to more emphasis on analysis and research related to recalls. In addition, the CPSC and other regulators should work with industry bodies to increase the responsiveness of the companies; the regulators need to play the role of facilitators.

Recalls and Consumers

While managers and regulators play an important and direct role in recalls, consumers can facilitate effective recalls by simply being aware of consumer product safety issues. In reality, the biggest impediment to product safety can perhaps be said to exist at the consumer end. This is not to say that consumers are to blame, but they do need to educate themselves about the changing nature of business and about the dynamics of consumer product safety.

One of the biggest consumer-held myths about product safety is the belief that if a product is for sale, it must have passed certain tests and received some kind of approval from an official body, such as a government regulator. Nothing could be further from the truth. In reality, very few products require approval from the government before they are sold. In fact, if we consider the number and range of products made and sold every day on the market, then the scale of regulation required to approve those products before they reach the market would be hundreds—if not thousands—of times more than the current size of the regulatory body. Not only is it infeasible for the government to approve and test products before they are sold, but it also runs counter to free market principles—requiring regulatory approval for every product would stifle innovation and entrepreneurship. This does not mean that products sold on the market are not tested at all, but simply that the government does not test them. Rather, the testing is left to the discretion of the company that sells the products. While this situation has been changing of late, with the CPSIA now mandating testing on certain products (primarily those used by children), a large number of products are still made and sold without mandatory testing of any kind.

In light of this, consumers need to educate themselves in order to guard against defective and potentially dangerous products. Consumers have several avenues open to them for tracking recall announcements. In particular, through the CPSC's mailing list, it is now easy for the public to receive e-mail alerts when products are recalled. By subscribing to such e-mail lists and returning recalled products, consumers can greatly improve the general safety of products in use.

Since a number of products are sold without being subjected to testing, consumers themselves should give the products they buy some degree of inspection. In most cases, this might be a simple visual inspection of the product's safety features. For example, a product could be examined for sharp edges, a tip-over hazard, or an entrapment hazard. However, in some cases, such as toys and children's products, the inspection might also need to include considerations of misuse and abuse before the products are given to a child. This does not mean an elaborate testing, but simply pulling, pinching, and pushing the product—just as a child might do. If the product does not withstand such testing, then it certainly does not belong in the hands of a child. On the other hand, if the product does withstand such testing, the chances of it being safe for children are somewhat higher.

Consumers are perhaps the most important link in consumer product safety because they can provide first-hand information about harmful incidents. Regulators and companies need this information in order to act and take preventive action. Therefore, it is important that consumers who become aware of incidents of actual or potential harm inform the involved companies as well as the regulators. In addition, consumers may also share such information on blogs and Web sites so that other users can be made aware of the issues on an ongoing basis. Such sharing can create an understanding of a specific problem related to a specific product, instead of assuming that each occurrence is simply an isolated incident. Careful consumers of the future need to spend more time and energy educating not only themselves but also their peers.

Not so long ago, a consumer typically bought a product made in one particular location and, in some cases, likely knew the maker of the product. In today's world of intertwined global supply chains, however, it is virtually impossible for a consumer to know who made a given product and what materials were used. While most products adhere to labeling requirements that provide the necessary information, currently companies are not required to list the sources of raw material and components. As a result, the information provided on the package is sketchy at best. Consumers need to be aware of both the complexity behind a simple product they have purchased and the potential for error in the enormous web of contractual relationships involved in that product's production. With this kind of awareness, consumers will be more cautious in their approach to product purchases and use, adopting a critical mindset rather than a naïve belief that the product was made in a straightforward fashion by one person in one company in one country.

While products sold on today's market may appear to be the same as they have always been, they have in fact been created within a complex web of relationships. Consumers need to educate themselves—and their fellow consumers—about this complexity and act in a more informed fashion.

Conclusion

Thanks to globalization, companies are now able to spread their value chain activities around the world. As a result, nearly every product sold on the market these days is a hybrid product—a product in which one or more of the value chain activities (design, raw material, components, assembly, manufacturing, or testing) has been conducted outside the country where the product will actually be sold. Along with this expansion of the value chain comes an increased risk of missteps in the making of a given product; an error at any stage of the value chain can lead to a product defect. When such defects pose harm to consumers, those products must be recalled.

The increased complexity of operations that bring a product to market is hidden from consumers and the general public, who often have no idea that the production process is so complex. Because of this naïveté, consumers and other stakeholders approach the issue of product recalls with a mindset that assumes the product was likely made by the company whose name appears on the packaging, and when a problem arises, the fault lies directly with that company. This perception is quite likely to change, however, when the product is made in a country the public holds in an unfavorable light. In such cases, consumers are likely to believe, or could be led to believe, that forces in the country of manufacture caused the problem. As a result, when a major recall of an imported product is issued, it is quite common for consumers and others to attribute the problem to that country as a whole.[14]

The practice of attributing a product defect to a specific country is problematic on two counts. First, in today's world, a product is rarely made in one country. Second, products are made by companies, not countries. It is true that conditions in a particular country may affect a number of products made by several companies within that country, so it is important to examine what went wrong with a given product before making such generalizations about the role of a country. In other words, we must examine the entire value chain process involved in making a product, including the location of each activity. Focusing only on the country of manufacture, or simply assuming that the problem lies with that country, can lead to misplaced blame.

The analysis in this book showed that toy recalls have increased in the recent past and that most of the recalls pertained to products made in China. But the analysis also shows that focusing only on China is inappropriate, since a large number of these recalls were a result of inadequate designs, for which China cannot fairly be blamed. While contract manufacturers in China may be responsible for manufacturing flaws, attributing all product failures to these parties may lead to incorrect conclusions and, hence, misplaced efforts to improve product safety. As the vast majority of product recalls are a result of design flaws, the greatest potential for improvement lies at the design end of the value chain.

Though design flaws have been and continue to be the major source of recalls, manufacturing flaws have also increased in the recent past. These manufacturing flaws have largely pertained to the presence of excess lead in surface paints, a systemic problem that existed in several developing countries, primarily in China. What was especially surprising about this particular issue was the length of time it took for companies to actually recognize the problem's extent and take action to correct it. Due to a lack of necessary inspection systems, the lead paint issue went unnoticed for years, finally surfacing in 2007, when the toy industry woke up to the massive nature of the problem.

We have also seen that a lack of organizational systems and experience can certainly contribute to recalls, as evidenced by the increase in recalls by retailers and distributors. Motivated by the low-cost operations in China, many retailers and distributors have begun to import products directly from China. As these companies do not possess the necessary understanding of the imported products and cannot adequately assess their flaws, recalls by retailers and distributors have increased. In addition, these organizations have found it particularly difficult to conquer the lead paint problem because they lack the necessary systems to monitor production and take corrective action.

While the problems with China's manufacturing practices have certainly contributed to recalls, they are not the only source of the recall wave. Over time, companies seem to have become less responsive to consumer safety issues, and this trend is reflected in the fact that the time to recall has become slower in the recent past. Also, companies appear to frequently recall products reactively, after the harm has been done to consumers, as opposed to recalling defective products in a preventive fashion. Finally, companies are now offering less remedy to consumers who return products, a scenario that has the potential to impede the effective recovery of the recalled products.

The complex operations involved in making products means that the issue of recalls should not be approached with a simplistic mindset. It is necessary to examine recalls critically to understand the reasons for them, to uncover what influences those reasons, and to learn how to prevent them. It is equally important to examine the responsiveness of the recalling companies to ensure that they conduct recalls promptly and thoroughly.

As today's products make their way to market through lengthy and complex global supply chains, managers need to ensure that the designs of their products are both sound and safe. In addition, they must see that the products are made according to their design specifications. Further, managers must make sure that products are properly assembled and correctly used by consumers. Inadequate attention to any of these aspects could directly result in defects and eventual recalls.

Researchers need to study the subject of product recalls from the perspective of consumers and society, as opposed to the organizational perspective that has been used until now. Taking a consumer perspective can help researchers to examine the recalls phenomenon more closely, rather than simply tallying up the numbers or determining the economic consequences of recalls to companies. Further, a more in-depth approach would identify the actual reasons for recalls as well as their non-economic consequences.

Regulators need to adopt a more analytical and facilitative approach rather than an administrative approach in this age of global supply chains. Regulators need to study the patterns among recalls. Then they can work with the industry to improve product safety through better designs and improve responsiveness through swiftly issued recalls and appropriate product recovery.

While managers, researchers, regulators, and consumers play an important role in ensuring product safety, there are other stakeholders that must be considered as well. These include the media, which provides information to the consumers, and the government, which lays down the policy framework. Just as consumers, regulators, researchers, and managers need to understand the complexity of today's hybrid products, every stakeholder should develop an appreciation for the changing nature of business and how this affects consumer safety. Such an appreciation, instead of the present practice of pointing fingers at developing countries, would help to improve product safety in the long run by enabling appropriate analysis and corrective action.

In conclusion, the analysis in this book has shown that the increases in product recalls may not have been caused by China (or any other country). Since a vast majority of products are recalled for design flaws and manufacturing flaw recalls (particularly for lead) have increased, all stakeholders must examine the issue of recalls in the proper perspective. In addition, the analysis has shown that companies have become less responsive in recent years, as reflected in slower recalls, reactive recalls, and less-motivating remedies. If consumer product safety goals are to be achieved, all interested parties should direct the necessary resources to prevent recalls and help companies act preventively when recalls are necessary, swiftly recalling products and providing an appropriate remedy that motivates consumers to return recalled products. In short, when it comes to managing recalls, it is important that *all stakeholders* take a critical approach so that consumer product safety can be improved.

Epilogue

Accelerating Cars, Contaminated Medicines, and Continuing Recalls

As someone who spends a lot of time researching recalls, I follow nearly every recall that is issued and safety problem that is reported. Beginning in late 2009, I began to notice that a number of safety problems were being reported that related specifically to Toyota vehicles and, specifically, to frame corrosion and unintended acceleration. The issue of unintended acceleration particularly caught my attention because the information reported in the media was sketchy, not to mention the serious danger the problem itself poses. Also, unintended acceleration has dogged many makes of models and cars over the years.

As a concerned consumer—my wife and I own a Toyota RAV4 that was later recalled—I decided to read all that I could in order to better understand the issue of unintended acceleration. I gathered that the problem had developed over time, with gas pedals not returning to their position or returning too slowly. I read that the vehicle's floor mats could be contributing to the problem, so to be on the safe side, I removed the floor mats from our vehicle and took the car out for a test drive to ensure that the brake and accelerator were working as they should.

On January 21, 2010, I read that Toyota had issued a recall of 2.3 million vehicles of several models, all due to sticking gas pedals that might cause unintended acceleration. Interestingly, Toyota had not yet developed a fix for this problem, and instead was simply asking drivers to apply firm pressure when breaking. As a recalls researcher, I found it strange that a recall was issued without a remedy. In the weeks to come, I followed the Toyota recall intently and was amazed at the number of issues that grew out of the original announcement, issues that were, in fact, very similar to the ones discussed in this book.

Recalls are not new, particularly in the auto industry, which often recalls more cars in a year than it sells.[1] Recalls for unintended acceleration are also nothing new; such complaints are often raised against auto manufacturers and sometimes involve recalls. The most notable case occurred in 1986, when, in response to a slew of complaints about unintended acceleration, 700 crashes, and six deaths, Audi recalled its sedans. The recall was made amidst a media frenzy (likely very similar to the one Toyota faced). Three years later, investigations by the NHTSA found that there was, in fact, nothing wrong with the cars; rather, the crashes had occurred due to possible pedal misapplication by drivers. In other words, that particular recall by Audi had been unnecessary. Since then, several sudden acceleration complaints and investigations have occurred, but in spite of all this attention, sudden unintended acceleration still remains a mystery. Nevertheless, the Toyota recalls of 2010 have proven to be highly instructive on many counts.

As soon as Toyota announced its recalls in January 2010, discussion in the U.S. media and the digital world revolved around how many U.S. citizens buy Japanese (foreign) cars in spite of their "inferiority" to American-made vehicles. The American media severely criticized Toyota, even though several large American (and other) automakers had also issued many recalls in the past. In fact, while the Toyota recall was unfolding, Ford completed a series of recalls that affected 14 million vehicles. Honda had recalled nearly 1.3 million vehicles over the course of three recalls; GM had recalled 1.3 million cars; and Nissan and Suzuki had recalled about half a million cars each. Yet, in spite of these facts, the initial focus of the Toyota uproar remained on the country of origin, just as it had in the case of so many other consumer product recalls.

This obsession with country of origin was taken further by a discussion about where the sticky pedals had, in fact, been made. The pedals in question were all made by CTS Corporation, which was an American company. Some argued that the pedals had likely been made according to Toyota's own designs, and that CTS was therefore not responsible for the recalls. This discussion died down as Toyota asserted that it alone was responsible for ensuring the safety of its vehicles, irrespective of who made the components. Even so, the issue of whether the sticky pedals were a result of a manufacturing flaw or a design flaw was far from resolved, and the NHTSA began investigations into cars of other makes that used CTS pedals.

A week after Toyota announced the recall, and several weeks after many more stories floated around the media about the sticky pedals, Toyota announced a fix that involved reinforcing the pedals. This fix, apparently approved by the NHTSA, became an issue in itself. Regulators expressed little confidence in Toyota's diagnosis of the problem and the solution offered, and asked Toyota to look into the possibility of malfunctioning electronics and software. Toyota asserted that it had no reason to believe that software problems were behind the unintended accelerations. Given the complexity of a car's make-up, it is very unlikely that the truth about this issue will be revealed any time soon.

As the confusion continued, several new reports highlighted that the number of sudden-acceleration complaints related to Toyota vehicles were the highest in the industry. In 2009, for example, 53 percent of sudden-acceleration complaints involved Toyota vehicles, compared to 34 percent for Volkswagen-Audi. However, when these figures are adjusted according to the number of cars sold by each company, Volkswagen-Audi tops the list with 11.5 complaints per 100,000 vehicles, followed by Toyota with 7.5, and BMW with 5.8. Further analysis of about 15,000 other complaints revealed that sudden-acceleration problems were an ongoing bane for many auto companies: Toyota's problems dated back to 2002; Volkswagen had a high rate of complaints, even though it used a brake override feature in its cars; and Honda had received many complaints in its 2001–2003 model years. Honda's rate of complaints has dropped in more recent years, in spite of the fact that the company does not use a brake override system.[2] From this, we can see that Toyota has not been the only company dealing with sudden-acceleration issues; however, due to the media circus that surrounded Toyota's recall, the company was being turned into a whipping post for the problem. This particular anecdote clearly shows the need to look at the data more critically, rather than simply counting the number of complaints against companies or the number of recalls companies issue.

While the focus of the Toyota recall initially fell on the country of origin, the same issue surfaced again in a more nuanced manner to explain why Toyota may be less responsive to its consumers, compared to other auto companies. The argument was that the Japanese government protects Toyota, and that governmental support, combined with Japan's weak consumer product safety standards, led to the conclusion that Toyota was in a position to place low emphasis on customer satisfaction. Supporters of this argument alleged that Toyota was not responsive to its customers in Japan and thus felt justified in being similarly unresponsive to its customers in other countries as well.[3]

One particular issue that sparked the indignation of all stakeholders was the amount of time Toyota took to announce its recall. While the exact extent of the delay on Toyota's part is still under investigation, in general, the sudden-acceleration complaints related to Toyota vehicles have seen an increase since 2002. More specifically, the complaints about sticky pedals had been known since at least April 2009, nearly nine months before Toyota issued a recall. As someone who has been researching the issue of the time to recall, I was very pleased to see questions being raised about the speed with which Toyota responded.[4] As recalls occur, it is important that questions be raised, not only about recalls as such, but also about the responsiveness of the companies themselves. After all, it is only through proactive and responsive behavior that companies can limit the damage from defective products. If companies respond only when such action becomes inevitable, untold damage can occur to consumers. Hence, all efforts should be made to ensure that companies act in a highly responsive manner, and public opinion certainly has a role to play in achieving that kind of corporate action. However, if consumers do not critically examine recalls and simply blame the country of manufacture, companies are less likely to be as responsive as they should be.

As the Toyota recall was publicly dissected, many of the company's internal practices also came to light. For example, it became known that Toyota estimated that it had saved $100 million by negotiating with regulators to limit a previous recall to 2007 Camry and Lexus models only. This information stemmed from an internal presentation made by Toyota's Washington office, perhaps to justify its own existence, and thus it may not correctly represent Toyota's overall approach. Even so, that such a presentation was made at all is cause for at least a small degree of concern. The concern increases in light of follow-up allegations (by a former Toyota attorney) of a cover-up at Toyota and consequent exhortations by a group vice president (in a leaked e-mail) that the company should come clean regarding mechanical failure in its gas pedals. Researching recalls is particularly challenging because companies do not share information and when they settle with affected consumers, they often bind them with non-disclosure clauses, which makes it even more difficult to gather the necessary information for research. Efforts by regulators and media to get to the bottom of the issue, even if off-the-mark at times, can help to unearth information that will be useful in gaining a better understanding of recalls and recalling companies.

The lack of responsiveness on Toyota's part was also evident in the initial refusal of Toyota's president, Akio Toyoda, to appear before a U.S. congressional hearing. In fact, it took Toyoda weeks to issue an apology over the gas-pedal issue. Faced with pressure from all sides, Toyoda finally appeared before the U.S. Congress, expressed regret for the inconvenience caused to drivers, and pledged full cooperation with the U.S. regulators. Some argued that Toyoda's initial reluctance to come out in the open and deal with the issue was reflective of a Japanese cultural norm in which senior managers remain in the background.

Even if the company president's lack of involvement could be overlooked, Toyota's communication with its customers was certainly far from effective. As an affected consumer, I know this to be true. For example, after weeks of reading about the sticking pedals, and ten days after the recall was announced, I received an e-mail from Toyota, which simply asked me to check the company's Web site for updates. This communication was followed a few weeks later by a letter, and then by another e-mail a few weeks after that from the dealer who had sold us our vehicle. Needless to say, these three communications from Toyota and its dealer paled in comparison to the dozens (if not hundreds) of news items I had been reading about the issue and about Toyota's mishandling of it. Since Toyota had my e-mail address (and those of its other customers), I would have been more at ease if I had heard directly from the company *before* any information from other sources had reached me. In fact, what makes auto recalls different from other recalls is that automakers possess the information that allows them to directly contact the car owners and implement the recall in a highly effective manner. In the case of other consumer products, companies do not know who bought the product and thus have to rely on consumer response in order to make the recall effective. However, despite possessing the necessary contact information, Toyota fell short in communicating with its customers.

While Toyota's tardy response was surprising, I was equally puzzled at my own heel-dragging in taking weeks to get the Toyota-suggested fix. Eventually I realized that my procrastination was understandable, since it was not clear whether the fix that Toyota had offered was, in fact, the right one. After all, the regulators had expressed doubt as to its appropriateness and had asked Toyota to examine its electronics as a possible alternative source of the problem. Further, Toyota's (and the NHTSA's) own behavior did not inspire confidence that the company had correctly identified the problem. Initially, Toyota and the NHTSA concluded that the car's floor mats interfered with the brake and gas pedals. Then it was found that all pedals made by CTS were likely to be sticky. Even this conclusion came into question when it was later alleged that a software malfunction could be the reason for the sudden acceleration problems.[5] Toyota's fix seemed unreliable when viewed within the larger context of the inconclusive investigations into the source of the problem and the conflicting reports about the usefulness of the proposed fix itself. While my own case may be an isolated one, it does serve to underscore the importance of knowing why consumers may or may not respond to recall notices. This kind of understanding allows the recalling company to arrive at a fix that appropriately motivates the affected consumers.

Toyota's lack of responsiveness was criticized not only by the U.S. government but also by the U.K. media, which pointed out that Toyota had not informed the U.K. government about the sticky-pedal issue until it was forced to do so. Further, the U.K. media criticized Toyota's lax response in informing its U.K. consumers about which models were affected and for the delay in announcing a remedy. I too have often wondered whether Toyota made only minimal attempts to contact me simply because I was not a U.S. consumer. These concerns and criticisms underscore the need for large multinational companies to adopt a uniform approach to recalls that would ensure a prompt and universal response to consumers across the globe. Otherwise, companies risk losing consumers in certain countries. This is an issue worthy of attention for researchers and practitioners of international business.

U.S. regulators criticized Toyota in an unprecedented manner. The language used against Toyota was harsh, ranging from calling Toyota "safety deaf," to warning people to "stop driving the cars," to announcing "they think they have a fix," and insisting that safety officials would "continue to hold Toyota's feet to the fire." Such criticism culminated in the U.S. Department of Transportation seeking a $16.4 million fine against Toyota for not reporting the defects promptly. This fine was the maximum possible under current legislation and was also the highest levied against any automaker in U.S. history. Not surprisingly, it became common to hear that the U.S. government was bullying Toyota because it had a major stake in Toyota's rivals, General Motors and Chrysler.[6]

As Toyota's recall played out, the company lost some of its market value. Its market share slipped from 17 percent in 2009 to 15.5 percent in the first four months of 2010. This drop is significant because Toyota had been gaining market share each year in recent memory. While the decrease in market share indicates an erosion of Toyota's brand equity, many of its existing consumers appear to be standing by Toyota. This may be due to the fact that these consumers have invested heavily in Toyota (through their car purchases) Toyota's failure would therefore drastically affect the resale value of these clients' vehicles. Alternatively, these consumers may simply have believed that Toyota vehicles were "fine" and that the U.S. government was unfairly hounding the company. In the case of low-value items such as toys, for example, it is easier for consumers to detach themselves from the issue (given their low investment); it is also easy for them to criticize the company that recalled the toys. In the larger-scale case of auto recalls, however, consumers may think that pointing their finger at a large company like Toyota may prove to be against their own best interests in the long run.

On June 4, 2010, Chrysler recalled about 35,000 Dodge Calibers to fix the sticky pedals in their vehicles. These pedals were also made by CTS. Thus, at least a part of the Toyota-bashing was less than necessary.

* * *

While there appears to be no end in sight for Toyota, yet another recall is making headlines as this work is being written. Johnson & Johnson has always enjoyed a stellar reputation for handling safety issues—a reputation earned in 1982 when it quickly recalled 31 million units of Tylenol after product tampering caused a few deaths. The cost of this recall to the company stood at over $100 million. Johnson & Johnson moved quickly to tamper-proof Tylenol's packaging and then reintroduced the (now-safer) product. Although Tylenol products stayed off the shelf for several weeks after the recall, the firm's prompt action helped the brand to regain its lost market share within nine months of the re-launch date. What was equally impressive was the fact that Johnson & Johnson managed to gain an unprecedented reputation for recall management.[7]

Ironically, the same Johnson & Johnson that turned a crisis into an opportunity to establish its reputation in 1982 now finds itself reeling under the burden of recalls in more recent times. Beginning in November 2009, the company announced four recalls. The latest, announced in May 2010, included 40 children's versions of Tylenol, Motrin, and Benadryl.[8] These products were recalled because of bacterial contamination, problems with ingredients, and the presence of tiny metal parts. In addition to its investigation into the harm these products have caused, the FDA issued a damning report of

its investigations into the conditions at the plant owned and operated by Johnson & Johnson in Fort Washington, Pennsylvania. Only
further investigations can shed any light on what truly went wrong
at Johnson & Johnson, which had remained the standard of recall
management for nearly three decades. It might be safe to conjecture,
however, that the systems and processes at the company were ineffec-
tive at identifying defects and that the company had likely become
less responsive to consumers.

* * *

Close on the heels of the Toyota and Johnson & Johnson recalls, a
few other large recalls were issued. On June 3, 20101, Maytag recalled
about 7 million dishwashers made in the United States that posed a
fire hazard due to an electrical failure in the dishwasher's heating ele-
ment. Maytag took more than four years to issue this recall, just as it
has with many of its recent recalls.[9] On the very next day, McDonald's
issued a recall of 12 million Shrek-themed glasses made in the United
States that contained cadmium. Surprisingly, McDonald's, which
escaped the lead recalls—due largely to its effective controls in
China—could not escape a recall of products made in its own backyard.[10] These two examples, just as the analysis in this book, illustrate
that poor manufacturing in China is not the sole cause of recalls.

* * *

Consumer product safety is an important, emotionally charged issue.
In the current days of global supply chains and multinational companies, mistakes can occur at any point in the value chain, as products
are designed, manufactured, and sold around the world. As a result,
it is often tempting for companies, consumers, and other stakeholders to identify *where* the product is made as the place to lay the blame
in the event of a product-safety issue. However, as the analysis in this
book has shown, pointing fingers at the country of manufacture does
nothing to improve product safety in general.

In order to understand what caused the defects and in turn arrive
at the appropriate corrective action, it is important to closely scrutinize the recall itself. More importantly, any analysis and figures presented to support a conclusion should be used very carefully, and
only after critically examining the multiple angles related to size of
the recall, the nature and severity of the problem, and the size of the
company issuing the recall.

While it is important to understand the nature and source of all defects, it is equally important to study the responsiveness of the company in terms of the time taken to issue a recall, the number of incidents that occurred before action was taken, and the remedy offered to recover the recalled products. The analysis in this book, combined with the recent examples of Toyota and Johnson & Johnson, show that companies appear to be increasingly less responsive on product safety in particular and to consumers in general. Therefore, research and regulatory effort focusing on the responsiveness of the company will not only yield insights about recalls, but will also encourage the recalling companies to be more responsive.

In addition to examining the reasons for recalls and the responsiveness of companies, it is also important to consider the reactions of consumers, which might range from outright rejection of the companies involved to unflinching loyalty to the same. Either reaction can pose an obstacle to effective recovery of products and thus to improving product safety in general.

In short, it is important that all stakeholders in consumer safety play their respective roles in an active and responsible manner by focusing less on the country of manufacture and more on the *reasons* for recall, *responsiveness* of companies, and *reactions* of consumers. Together, these three dimensions will boost the effective handling of recalls. Even more importantly, they will improve consumer product safety in general.

Appendix

Toyota's Troubles—A Timeline

February 2004—State Farm Insurance notifies the National Highway Traffic Safety Administration (NHTSA) of increased claims of "unintended acceleration" for 2002 and 2003 model year Lexus ES300s and Toyota Camrys.

February 2004—The NHTSA begins an investigation into electronic throttle control malfunction complaints in 2002 and 2003 model year Lexus ES300s. In July 2004, the investigation is closed with no defects found.

December 31, 2004—Toyota vehicles represent 20 percent of total unintended acceleration complaints in 2004. This represents an increase of 4 percent from 2000. Toyota's U.S. market share in 2004 was 12.2 percent compared to 9.3 percent in 2000.

April 2005—The NHTSA investigates 2002–2005 model year Toyota Camry, Lexus ES, and Solara vehicles for an electronic cause of the unintended acceleration, but closes the investigation in January 2006 with no evidence of a defect.

October 2005—Toyota recalls 1.41 million vehicles for defective headlight switching systems.

March 2007—Toyota receives five complaints against its 2007 Lexus ES350 vehicles for unintended acceleration, as well as problems with its Tundra model. Toyota begins investigation. The NHTSA begins similar investigation and identifies the floor mats as the problem in preliminary analysis.

July 26, 2007—A driver is killed in San Jose, California, after his car is rammed by a 2007 Toyota Camry; the Camry driver is seriously hurt.

September 13, 2007—The NHTSA finds the floor mats catching the gas pedal as the cause of the crash in San Jose in July and notifies Toyota that a recall is required.

September 26, 2007—The company recalls 55,000 floor mats in its 2007 and 2008 model year Camrys and Lexus ES350s.

October 2007—*Consumer Reports* magazine removes three Toyota vehicles from its safety recommendation list, stating that "after years of sterling reliability, Toyota is showing cracks in its armor."

April 2008—The NHTSA begins investigation on 2004 Sienna minivans and 2004–2008 model year Tacoma trucks for unintended acceleration.

April 19, 2008—The crash of a 2005 Camry into a tree due to "out of control acceleration" causes the death of its driver. The vehicle does not have the floor mats that were seen as the cause of accidents pertaining to the previous recall. A lawsuit alleged that the software controlling the vehicle's systems is flawed. Toyota denies the allegations.

June 2008—Toyota states, in regard to accelerator complaints, that "while accelerator pedal feeling could change under certain conditions, Toyota considered it to be a driver-ability issue unrelated to safety."

January 2009—Toyota recalls 1.3 million vehicles for vehicle and seatbelt defects and 26,501 Siennas for a floor carpet defect.

April 27, 2009—Reports from Ireland about sticking pedals are sent to engineers at Toyota in Los Angeles.

July 2009—Toyota "estimates that it saved $100 million by negotiating with regulators to limit a previous recall to 2007 Toyota Camry and Lexus ES models for sudden acceleration."

August 28, 2009—A 2009 Lexus ES350 travelling 120+ mph crashes in Santee, California, killing a family of four. The 911 call from a passenger in the car before the vehicle crashes states that the gas pedal was stuck. It is believed the pedal may have been caught in the floormat.

August 2009—Toyota recalls 690,000 vehicles in China for a defect in window stitching.

September 29, 2009—The NHTSA informs Toyota that it needs to recall defective pedals in its vehicles. Toyota announces a 3.8 million vehicle recall for the removal of floor mats that could catch accelerator pedals, causing unintended acceleration. Offers "safe" replacements, while recommending that consumers remove the mats until the company can fix the problem. Recall involves most Toyota vehicles from 2007 to 2010, as well as Toyota Prius models from 2004 to 2010.

November 25, 2009—Toyota expands its recall to 4.26 million vehicles, stating it will reconfigure the length of its gas pedals, install a brake override system, and redesign its floor mats. Vehicles recalled now include 2007–2010 Camry and Tundra models, 2005–2010 Avalons, and more Lexus models.

December 26, 2009—A Toyota Avalon crashes into a pond after speeding off a road, killing four people. Police report that they found floor mats, the stated cause for the unintended acceleration, in the trunk.

December 28, 2009—In New Jersey, a driver drove his speeding, uncontrollable 2007 Avalon to a dealership by shifting in and out of neutral. Once parked, the motor was still running and the tires/brakes began to smoke.

January 16, 2010—Toyota tells the NHTSA that its pedals manufactured by CTS Corporation have a defect that can make them become stuck.

January 21, 2010—Toyota recalls 2.3 million vehicles (2005–2010 Camrys and Tundras; 2008–2010 Sequoias; 2009–2010 Rav4s, Corrollas, Matrixes; 2010 Highlanders; 2009–2010 Pontiac Vibes) for sticking gas pedals that may cause unintended acceleration. Toyota recommended that drivers use firm pressure when braking until they can fix their vehicles.

January 26, 2010—Toyota stops selling its defective models and ceases production for a week in February.

January 27, 2010—Toyota adds 1.1 million vehicles to the recall involving floor mats (2008–2010 Highlanders, 2009–2010 Corollas, 2009–2010 Venzas, 2009–2010 Matrixes, 2009–2010 Pontiac Vibes).

January 28, 2010—Toyota announces it will recall an indeterminate number of vehicles in Europe and 75,000 RAV4s in China for the gas pedal defect.

January 28, 2010—The NHTSA approves Toyota's pedal fix.

January 29, 2010—Toyota announces recalls of 1.8 million vehicles in Europe.

February 2, 2010—The U.K.'s *Guardian* reports that U.K. drivers will have to wait a few weeks before they are able to know whether their vehicle has a defective accelerator pedal.

February 2, 2010—The NHTSA restarts its investigation into Toyota's electric throttle control system. Transportation Secretary Ray LaHood states, "While Toyota is taking responsible action now, it unfortunately took an enormous effort to get to this point." He calls Toyota "a little safety deaf."

February 3, 2010—The Japanese government orders Toyota to investigate braking problems with its 2010 Prius. The NHTSA states that it has received 124 complaints against the Prius's braking.

February 3, 2010—Ray LaHood recommends that Toyota drivers who own a car with potential defects to "stop driving it," although later that morning, he rescinds his comments, explaining they were a misstatement.

February 3, 2010—Toyota announces it has sent information of 180,865 recalled vehicles to the United Kingdom's auto licensing office. Toyota states that the repair should take only 30 minutes at a service center.

February 4, 2010—Toyota identifies a flaw with the 2010 Prius's braking systems and states that it is a software error—Prius vehicles built since January already have been modified. The NHTSA announces investigation into 2010 model year Prius vehicles. The number of recalled vehicles reaches 8.1 million. Toyota estimates that it will lose $2 billion from costs associated with the recalls.

February 5, 2010—President of Toyota, Akio Toyoda, makes a public apology at a Japanese news conference for the problems associated with its vehicles. Toyoda announces he is creating a task force to investigate quality issues and that the company is deciding whether to make another Prius recall. This is amidst reports by the *Guardian* that Toyota was aware of the accelerator fault in the winter of 2008–2009 but had originally identified it not as a safety problem but as a quality problem, and did not inform the U.K. government until ordered to do so.

February 9, 2010—Toyota recalls 437,000 hybrid vehicles (2010 Prius's, Sais, Prius PHVs, and Lexus HS250hs) for a problem with their regenerative breaking system.

February 12, 2010—8,000 Toyota 2010 Tacoma trucks are recalled for front propeller shaft issues. The front propeller could malfunction, potentially affecting vehicle control.

February 16, 2010—Toyota states that it will stop production at two of its plants due to decreased sales from the recalls; The NHTSA orders the company to provide evidence as to when it knew of the defects in its vehicles.

February 17, 2010—President Akio Toyoda begins rebuilding the company's tarnished image by introducing new safety measures, such as more prompt defect notification and mandatory brake override systems in future models (something that many German automakers already do). The NHTSA announces it will investigate steering issues in 500,000 Corollas.

February 22, 2010—Politicians on the U. S. House of Representatives Energy and Commerce Committee assert that Toyota used a faulty study to assess whether there was a software issue with its unintended acceleration problems. They further assert that the company made deceptive comments about the recalls. Toyota is subpoenaed by a federal grand jury of the Southern District of New York for documents pertaining to unintended acceleration and disclosure policies.

February 23, 2010—*Consumer Reports* takes two Toyota cars off of its "Top Pick" list due to their halt in sales because of the recall. Congressional hearing witnesses identify software issues as the cause for unintended acceleration in some Toyota vehicles. Jim Lentz, COO of Toyota USA, states the company is still investigating whether there is an electronics issue in its vehicles' accelerator pedals.

February 24, 2010—After U.S. pressure, Toyota president Akio Toyoda appears before a U.S. congressional hearing, stating, "I'm deeply sorry for any accident that Toyota drivers have experienced" and pledging full cooperation from Toyota.

March 4, 2010—The NHTSA announces that it is investigating recalled Toyotas that were repaired, after receiving 60 complaints of unintended acceleration from them. Toyota suggests that these vehicles may not have been repaired properly.

April 5, 2010—The U.S. Department of Transportation announces that it will pursue a $16.4 million fine of Toyota (the maximum allowed under current legislation) for failing to notify the government of the defects within the allowed time frame. It is the largest fine against an automaker in U.S. history.

April 13, 2010—Toyota's luxury division, Lexus, stops the sale of its 2010 Lexus GX460 vehicles when *Consumer Reports* magazine tells potential buyers that the vehicle has an increased chance of roll-overs and steering control issues.

April 16, 2010—Toyota recalls 870,000 Sienna vehicles (2008–2010 models) due to a cable holding the rear-mounted spare tire potentially corroding from road salt. This could cause the tire to fall onto the road while driving.

April 19, 2010—Toyota agrees to pay the $16.4 million fine from the U.S. Department of Transportation. Toyota recalls 10,000 Lexus GX460 vehicles that *Consumer Reports* magazine warned buyers against, stating that the issue is with the electronic stability control system.

April 28, 2010—Toyota recalls 50,000 Sequoia vehicles due to "low-speed acceleration" issues with its electronic stability system.

Notes

Prologue

1. CPSC, "Infant Entrapment and Suffocation Prompts Stork Craft to Recall More Than 2.1 Million Drop-Side Cribs," November 23, 2009, http://www.cpsc.gov/cpscpub/prerel/prhtml10/10046.html.
2. CPSC, "Aqua-Leisure Industries Recalls Inflatable Pool Ladders for Fall Hazard," May 17, 2006, http://www.cpsc.gov/cpscpub/prerel/prhtml06/06165.html.

1 2007: The Year of the Recall

1. W. Bogdanich and J. Hooker, "From China to Panama, a Trail of Poisoned Medicine," *New York Times*, May 6, 2007, http://www.nytimes.com/2007/05/06/world/americas/06poison.html.
2. In early 2008, Panamanian investigators concluded that at least 115 people had been killed by the counterfeit cold medicine. The actual number of victims was likely much higher because not all cases, particularly those from rural areas, would have been reported to the health authorities. For further details, please see W. Bogdanich, "Panama Releases Report on '06 Poisoning," *New York Times*, February 14, 2008, http://www.nytimes.com/2008/02/14/world/americas/14panama.htm.
3. D. Barboza and A. Barrionuevo, "In China, Additive to Animals' Food is an Open Secret," *New York Times*, April 30, 2007, http://www.nytimes.com/2007/04/30/business/worldbusiness/30food.html. In a rare case, a U.S. company also used melamine in its animal feed. Please see A. Martin, "Melamine from U.S. Put in Feed," *New York Times*, May 31, 2007, http://www.nytimes.com/2007/05/31/business/31food.html.
4. For a rich and detailed account of the pet food recalls, please see M. Nestle, *Pet Food Politics: The Chihuahua in the Coal Mine* (Berkeley: University of California Press, 2008).
5. Please see company Web site for further details: www.foregintire.com.

6. A. Martin, "Chinese Tires are Ordered Recalled," *New York Times*, May 26, 2007, http://www.nytimes.com/2007/06/26/business/worldbusiness/26tire.html.

7. D. Barboza, "Chinese Tire Maker Rejects U.S. Charge of Defects," *New York Times*, May 26, 2007, http://www.nytimes.com/2007/06/26/business/worldbusiness/26iht-tires.1.6335169.html.

8. In 2009, China and the United States were locked in a dispute about tire tariffs. Please see L. Chiang and L. Hornby, "China says data shows U.S. tire tariff not fair," *Reuters*, September 15, 2009, http://www.reuters.com/article/idUSTRE58E1CB20090915.

9. The regulatory limit for lead was later reduced to 0.009 percent on August 14, 2009. Please see for further details Consumer Product Safety Commision, "RC2 Corp. to Pay $1.25 Million Civil Penalty," December 29, 2009, http://www.cpsc.gov/cpscpub/prerel/prhtml10/10094.html.

10. B. Dorfman, "Consumer last to know about Mattel toy recall," *Reuters*, August 2, 2007, http://www.reuters.com/article/domesticNews/idUSN0230401920070802 and L., "After Stumbling, Mattel Cracks Down in China," *New York Times*, August 29, 2007, http://www.nytimes.com/2007/08/29/business/worldbusiness/29mattel.html.

11. M. Ryan, "POLL—One in four Americans 'very worried' by China imports," *San Diego Union—Tribune*, September 19, 2007, http://www.signonsandiego.com/news/nation/20070919-0400-usa-foodsafety-poll.html.

12. S. Labaton, "Bigger Budget? No, Responds Safety Agency," *New York Times*, October 30, 2007, http://www.nytimes.com/2007/10/30/washington/30consumer.html.

13. M. Felcher, *It's No Accident: How Corporations Sell Dangerous Baby Products* (Monroe, ME: Common Courage Press, 2001).

14 The discussion on global toy industry and the aftermath of recalls was excerpted from Bapuji H, Beamish P. 2008. Mattel and the Toy Recalls. Cases A and B with permission from Ivey Publishing.

15. CBC News, "China recalls leukemia drugs, rejects North American meat exports," September 17, 2007, http://www.cbc.ca/consumer/story/2007/09/17/china-exports.html and "China rejects U.S. imports of pulp, apricots for contamination," June 26, 2007, http://www.cbc.ca/consumer/story/2007/06/26/china-trade.html.

16. For an in-depth account of global supply chains in the textile industry, please see P. Rivoli. *The travels of a t-shirt in the global economy: An economist examines the markets, power, and politics of world trade.* New Jersey:John Wiley and Sons. 2nd edition. 2009 and R. L. Snyder. *Fugitive Denim: A Moving Story of People and Pants in the Borderless World of Global Trade.*New York: W.W. Norton.

17. Peng, M., & Chen, H. 2011. Strategic responses to domestic and foreign institutional pressures in the Chinese toy industry. International Studies of Management and Organization (In Press).

2 Toy Recalls: Up, Up, and Up

1. CPSC, "CPSC Overview," http://www.cpsc.gov/about/about.html.
2. CPSC, *2009 Performance and Accountability Report,* http://www.cpsc.gov/cpscpub/pubs/reports/2009par.pdf.
3. CPSC, "RC2 Corp. Recalls Various Thomas & Friends™ Wooden Railway Toys Due to Lead Poisoning Hazard," June 13, 2007, http://www.cpsc.gov/cpscpub/prerel/prhtml07/07212.html.
4. CPSC, "Target Recalls Dive Sticks Due to Impalement Hazard," November 19, 2008, http://www.cpsc.gov/cpscpub/prerel/prhtml09/09048.html.
5. CPSC, "Evenflo Recalls Telephone Toys Due to Choking Hazard," July 16, 2009, http://www.cpsc.gov/cpscpub/prerel/prhtml09/09275.html.
6. CPSC, "Fitness Balls Recalled by EB Brands Due to Fall Hazard; New Assembly Instructions Provided," April 16, 2009, http://www.cpsc.gov/CPSCPUB/PREREL/prhtml09/09196.html.
7. It may be noted that all these injuries are not necessarily caused by toys. These injuries are associated with toys and may have occurred during the course of play. For further details, please see S. Garland, "Toy-Related Deaths and Injuries Calendar Year 2008," http://www.cpsc.gov/library/toymemo08.pdf.
8. CPSC, "CPSC Warns of Toy Chest Hazard," February 25, 1974, http://www.cpsc.gov/cpscpub/prerel/prhtml74/74013.html.
9. It could be argued that a toy chest is not a toy. However, the data in this book uses the categorizations made by the CPSC, which is more likely to have classified the recalls into certain categories, following sound logic. It is not our intention to make newer categorizations or to discuss the appropriateness of each categorization. We simply use the data from the CPSC Web site to analyze issues related to the recalls.
10. The number of recalls in each year presented in this book and those in other works relying on the CPSC data may not exactly match, particularly because the CPSC uses a different time frame for each year. This book uses the CPSC raw data to compute the recalls issued in each calendar year, running from January to December. In contrast, the CPSC uses a different budget year that runs from October to September.
11. CPSC, "Children's Stuffed Toys Recalled By Daiso Due to Choking Hazard," July 25, 2008, http://www.cpsc.gov/cpscpub/prerel/prhtml08/08597.html and CPSC, "Snap Beads Recalled By Edushape Due to Choking Hazard," December 8, 2009, http://www.cpsc.gov/cpscpub/prerel/prhtml10/10709.html.

12. CPSC, "CPSC Announces Recall of Metal Toy Jewelry Sold in Vending Machines," July 8, 2004, http://www.cpsc.gov/cpscpub/prerel/prhtml04/04174.html.

13. CPSC, "CPSC, Brand Imports, LLC Announce Recall of Children's Rings," March 2, 2004, http://www.cpsc.gov/cpscpub/prerel/prhtml04/04090.html.

14. CPSC, "CPSC, Firms Announce Swimming Pool Dive Stick Recall Because of Impalement Risk to Children," June 24, 1999, http://www.cpsc.gov/cpscpub/prerel/prhtml99/99127.html.

15. Y. Luo, "A Strategic Analysis of Product Recalls: The Role of Moral Degradation and Organizational Control," *Management and Organization Review*, 4(2):183–196.

16. J. Barney and S. Zhang, "Trusting the Chinese Brand," *Management and Organization Review*, 4(2).

17. M. B. Teagarden, "Learning from Toys: Reflections on the 2007 Recall Crisis," *Thunderbird International Business Review*, 51(1).

18. M. Lyles, B. Flynn, and M. Frohlich, "All Supply Chains Don't Flow Through: Understanding Supply Chain Issues in Product Recalls," *Management and Organization Review*, 4(2).

19. M. Peng and H. Chen, "Strategic Responses to Domestic and Foreign Institutional Pressures in the Chinese Toy Industry," *International Studies of Management and Organization* (2011).

3 Toy Recalls and China: The Twain that Always Meet?

1. Bapuji H, Beamish P, Laplume A. 2007. "Toy Import and Recall Levels: Is there a connection?" *Research Reports*, November. Asia Pacific Foundation of Canada.

2. This data was downloaded on April 10, 2010.

3. G. Linden, K. L. Kraemer, and J. Dedrick, "Who Captures Value in a Global Innovation System? The Case of Apple's iPod," University of California at Irvine, Personal Computing Industry Center (PCIC) working paper, June 2007.

4. Bapuji et al., 2007. Op. Cit.

5. J. Ferman, "Dolls, Toys, Games, and Children's Vehicles" (NAICS Code 33993), U.S. Department of Commerce Industry Report, March 4, 2009, http://www.ita.doc.gov/td/ocg/toyoutlook_09.pdf.

4 China's Toy Recalls: The High Cost of Low Price?

1. CPSC, "CPSC, Firms Announce Swimming Pool Dive Stick Recall Because of Impalement Risk to Children," June 24, 1999, http://www.cpsc.gov/cpscpub/prerel/prhtml10/10132.html.

2. CPSC,. "Weight Watchers Recalls Plush Hungry Figures and Magnets Due to Puncture Hazard," August 20, 2009, http://www.cpsc.gov/cpscpub/prerel/prhtml09/09318.html.

3. The proportions of low- and high-priced toys recalled do not sum up to 100 percent because some recall notices do not provide price information and were thus excluded from this analysis.

4. The discussion in this section only focuses on low-priced toy recalls for the purposes of brevity. Further, the high-priced toy recalls are simply the opposite of low-priced toy recalls, in general. Therefore, the patterns for low-priced recalls are the opposite of those for high-priced toy recalls.

5 Toys Made in China, but Designed in…?

1. G. M. Grossman and E. Rossi-Hansberg, E., "The rise of Offshoring: It's Not Wine for Cloth Anymore," *Proceedings of the Federal Reserve Bank of Kansas City*, 2006, 59–102.
2. P. Guinaudeau, "Toy Markets in the World," NPD Group, 2009 Edition, Australia.
3. D. Barboza, "China Bars Two Companies From Exporting Toys," *New York Times*, August, 10, 2007, http://query.nytimes.com/gst/fullpage.html?res=9405EED91030F933A2575BC0A9619C8B63&sec=&spon=.
4. J. Ferman, *Toy Industry Outlook 2009*, report prepared for the U.S. Department of Commerce, March 4, 2009, http://www.ita.doc.gov/td/ocg/toyoutlook_09.pdf.
5. Source: U.S. Census Bureau.
6. Ferman, *Toy Industry Outlook 2009*, 2 http://www.ita.doc.gov/td/ocg/toyoutlook_09.pdf.
7. E. Johnson and T. Clock, "Mattel, Inc: Vendor Operations in Asia," Tuck School of Business at Dartmouth case study.
8. CPSC under Section 16 CFR 1115.13(d)
9. Bapuji H, Beamish P. 2007. Toy Recalls: Is China Really the Problem? *Canada-Asia Commentary*, September. Asia Pacific Foundation of Canada.
10. CPSC, "CPSC, Mattel, Inc. Announce Recall of BATMAN™ BATMOBILE™ Toy Vehicle," April 14,2004, http://www.cpsc.gov/cpscpub/prerel/prhtml04/04118.html.
11. CPSC, "CPSC Saves Lives Through Voluntary Efforts and Oversight: Making Hair Dryers Safer," May 5, 1996, http://www.cpsc.gov/CPSCPUB/PUBS/SUCCESS/dryers.html.
12. CPSC, "Hair Dryers Recalled by Vintage International Due to Electrocution Hazard," June 3, 2009, http://www.cpsc.gov/cpscpub/prerel/prhtml09/09235.html; CPSC, "Hair Dryers Recalled by Universalink International Trading Due to Electrocution Hazard," April 29, 2009, http://www.cpsc.gov/cpscpub/prerel/prhtml09/09205.html;CPSC, "Hair Dryers Recalled By Big Lots Stores, Inc. Due to Electrocution Hazard," March 11, 2009, http://www.cpsc.gov/cpscpub/prerel/prhtml09/09147.html. All three recalls were issued by three importing companies in the United States. These hair dryers were made in China, Thailand, and Taiwan.
13. CPSC, "Dive Sticks," *Code of Federal Regulations*, Vol. 16, part 1500, March 7, 2001, http://www.cpsc.gov/BUSINFO/frnotices/fr01/divestik.html and CPSC, "Swim 'N Score Dive Sticks Recalled by

Modell's Due to Risk of Impalement Injury to Children," November 13, 2008, http://www.cpsc.gov/cpscpub/prerel/prhtml09/09043.html.

14. CPSC, "Maclaren USA Recalls to Repair Strollers Following Fingertip Amputations," November 9, 2009, http://www.cpsc.gov/cpscpub/prerel/prhtml10/10033.html.

15. CPSC, "Graco Recalls Strollers Due to Fingertip Amputation and Laceration Hazards," January 20, 2010, http://www.cpsc.gov/cpscpub/prerel/prhtml10/10115.html; CPSC, "Regal Lager Announces Recall to Repair CYBEX Strollers; Risk of Fingertip Amputation and Laceration Hazards," January 27, 2010, http://www.cpsc.gov/cpscpub/prerel/prhtml10/10123.html; CPSC, "Britax Recalls Strollers Due to Risk of Fingertip Amputations and Lacerations," February 10, 2010, http://www.cpsc.gov/cpscpub/prerel/prhtml10/10137.html.

16. CPSC, "CPSC, Pokémon USA Announce Recall of Pokémon Plush Toys," July 8, 2005, http://www.cpsc.gov/cpscpub/prerel/prhtml05/05222.html.

17. CPSC, "Fisher-Price Recalls Learning Pots and Pans™ Toys Due to Choking Hazard," August 7, 2008, http://www.cpsc.gov/CPSCPUB/PREREL/prhtml08/08362.html.

18. CPSC, "Playskool Voluntarily Recalls Toy Tool Benches after the Death of Two Toddlers," September 22, 2006, http://www.cpsc.gov/cpscpub/prerel/prhtml06/06266.html.

19. CPSC, "CPSC, Toys"R"Us Announce Recall of Children's Soap Craft Set," December 24, 1997, http://www.cpsc.gov/cpscpub/prerel/PRHTML98/98049.html.

20. CPSC, "Aqua-Leisure Industries Recalls Inflatable Pool Ladders for Fall Hazard," May 17, 2006, http://www.cpsc.gov/cpscpub/prerel/prhtml06/06165.html and http://www.aqualeisure.com/site/index.php?id=69.

21. CPSC, "GE Recalls to Inspect and Repair Wall Ovens Due to Fire and Burn Hazards," November 18, 2008, http://www.cpsc.gov/cpscpub/prerel/prhtml09/09046.html and General Electric, "GE Wall Oven—November 2008 Recall," http://www.geappliances.com/products/recall/wall_oven_08/faq.htm.

22. Coding for the flaw type based on product recall notices is a difficult task because the notices do not give sufficient information about the processes behind the recall. The notices are crafted carefully (often with the involvement of lawyers from recalling companies) to avoid future litigation. Nevertheless, it is possible to infer in most cases if the product recall was likely due to a flaw in design or manufacturing. Design flaw is systemic and affects the entire product as opposed to a few items (or a few batches of production). In contrast, manufacturing flaw is a deviation from original product plan and specifications.

Therefore, the following rules can be applied to infer if a recall was due to a design or a manufacturing flaw in the product:

- Is the problem/problematic component likely an integral part of the original product plan and specifications? For example, small parts that are detachable or become detached during use are an integral part of the original product plan. In contrast, lead paint or needles in stuffed toys could not conceivably be designed into the products.Is the problem a result of non-adherence to standards and regulations that describe safety features? Is it a deviation from standards or likely a deviation from specifications?
- Could the problem/problematic component have been reasonably identified during routine inspections (that are likely to have taken place)? In other words, is it reasonable to expect that the company selling the product could have realized (with relative ease) that it was not as per specifications?
- Did the company recall a few batches manufactured during a short period of time or the entire production? In the former case, the problem likely occurred during manufacturing and might not have been noted during inspections (or simply fell through the cracks). In other words, the problem was not inherent to the product but to the production on a few days.
- Did the company offer a replacement of the same product or one of the following: refund, store coupon, retrofit repair kit? If the same product is offered, it indicates that the product itself was not problematic but certain units were affected. So, the remedy was to offer the same product produced on different dates. If a retrofit repair kit was provided, it is likely that the problem was not initially envisaged but was addressed by adding components that would eliminate the hazard (for example, cap to close a gap or covers to ensure that sharp parts are not reachable). Refund would mean that the entire product line was likely problematic.
- Did the recall notice (or related Web sites) mention specifically if it was a manufacturing or a design problem? Did the recall notice mention which batches of similar/same products are not recalled and why? What is different between the recalled and not recalled products: is it improved design?
- Did the recall notice refer to a redesigned product, sold now or offered as a replacement for the recalled product?

Although most of the recall notices could be coded with the help of above rules, in some cases it is not possible to code based on the information given because the problem could have been either manufacturing or design. For example, seam separation and the resultant small beads falling off the toys could arguably be the result of either the seam (design) or manufacturing (easy separation). In some cases, it is difficult to tell—for example, the nozzle coming off unexpectedly from a water gun. These are coded as "Not Sure."

23. CPSC, "CPSC Announces Recalls Of Imported Crayons Because Of Lead Poisoning Hazard," April 5, 1994, http://www.cpsc.gov/cpsc-pub/prerel/prhtml94/94055.html.

24. J. Crow, "Why Use Lead in Paint?" report for the Royal Society of Chemistry, August 21, 2007, http://www.rsc.org/chemistryworld/News/2007/August/21080701.asp.

25. T. Gruca, "MN Child Dies Of Lead Poisoning; Bracelet Blamed," CBS, March 23, 2006, http://wcco.com/topstories/Reebok.Minneapolis.lead.2.356513.html. Following the death of Jarnell Brown, the CPSC and Reebok recalled 300,000 units of the jewelry distributed by Reebok with its shoes.

6 More Players and More Recalls

1. Mattel, *Mattel Annual Report 2009,* http://corporate.mattel.com/annual-report/assets/pdf/MattelAnnualReport2009.pdf.

2. A. Drury, "Concerns about China-made Toys Hurt Holiday Sales," *The Journal News,* January 2008.

3. R.S. Lazich, *Market Share Reporter* (Farmington Hills, MI: Gale Group, 2004).

4. K. Nolan, "Toys'R'Us Not Playing Games With Success," *Retailing Today* 46, no. 13 (September 10, 2007): 24.

5. D. Desjardins, "Target to Leapfrog over Toys'R'Us into No. 2 Spot," *Retailing Today* 45, no. 7 (2006): 36.

6. CPSC, "Dunkin' Donuts Recalls Glow Sticks Due to Choking and Strangulation Hazards," October 17, 2007, http://www.cpsc.gov/cpscpub/prerel/prhtml08/08030.html; CPSC, "State Farm® Recalls Good Neigh Bears® Due to Choking Hazard," March 17, 2009, http://www.cpsc.gov/cpscpub/prerel/prhtml09/09156.html; CPSC, "CPSC, Gateway Announce Recall of Foam Rubber Toy Cows," October 8, 1999, http://www.cpsc.gov/cpscpub/prerel/prhtml00/00002.html.

7. Although the recall notices indicate the type of company, we realized that this categorization was not consistent because the same companies were listed as manufacturers in some and importers in others. Therefore, we conducted extensive searches to collect data on the business activities of each company in our sample. We collected information about the business operations of the recalling company from their industry codes in Compustat. For privately listed firms, we checked in the Dun and Bradstreet directory, as well as with Hoovers and on the companies' own Web sites.

8. In recent years Hasbro has closed nearly all its manufacturing facilities and relied on contract manufacturers. However, during our relatively

long study period, Hasbro maintained factories and, more importantly, continues to design its own toys. Therefore, we coded Hasbro as a manufacturer. Mattel not only designs toys but also maintains its own manufacturing facilities where nearly 50 percent of the toys sold by Mattel are made. For the remaining half, Mattel relies on contract manufacturers. The manufacturing facilities of Mattel exist in several countries, including China.

9. Our categorization was a subjective exercise since it involved reading information about a company and assigning an appropriate code. In order to ensure that the categorization was reliable, a member of the research team and a graduate student coded the variable independently. The agreement level between the coders was 91.3 percent. We computed Cohen's Kappa to estimate the reliability of the coding and found that the coding was highly reliable (Kappa = 0.82 and p < 0.001). Following this, the companies on which the coders could not agree were discussed and resolved, which resulted in a complete agreement over the categorization.

10. CPSC, "Target Recalls Dive Sticks Due to Impalement Hazard," November 28, 2008, http://www.cpsc.gov/cpscpub/prerel/prhtml09/09048.html.

11. CPSC,. 16 CFR Part 1500. *CPSC*. March 7. Available from: http://www.cpsc.gov/BUSINFO/frnotices/fr01/divestik.html

12. CPSC, "Swim 'N Score Dive Sticks Recalled by Modell's Due to Risk of Impalement Injury to Children," November 13, 2008, http://www.cpsc.gov/cpscpub/prerel/prhtml09/09043.html; CPSC, "CPSC, Dollar General Corp. Announce Recall of Dive Sticks," February 16, 2005, http://www.cpsc.gov/cpscpub/prerel/prhtml05/05112.html.

13 For an article on Creata, the company that makes toys for companies like McDonald's and Kellogg's, please see: J. Ogando. "These Toy Engineers Don't Play Around," *Design News*, October 22, 2006, http://www.designnews.com/article/11809-These_Toy_Engineers_Don_t_Play_Around.php

14. D. Barboza and L. Story, "Mattel Issues New Recall of Toys Made in China," *New York Times*, August 14, 2007, http://www.nytimes.com/2007/08/14/business/15toys-web.html.

7 Slow to React in a Fast-Paced World

1. The databases of National Highway Traffic Safety Administration (NHTSA) provide detailed information on defect investigations, such as when the information was received, what investigation was conducted, what conclusion was arrived at, and what action was taken. As part of the recent changes in the regulation, the CPSC is making efforts to make this information publicly available.

2. CPSC, "Gund Recalls to Replace Baby Books Due to Choking Hazard," April 6, 2010, http://www.cpsc.gov/cpscpub/prerel/prhtml10/10190.html.

3. P. Callahan, "Inside the Botched Recall of a Dangerous Toy," *Chicago Tribune,* May 7, 2007, http://www.chicagotribune.com/news/watchdog/chi-safety-magnets2-story,0,5313514,full.story and "Long Trail of Warnings on Magnets," *Chicago Tribune,* news graphic, http://www.chicagotribune.com/news/watchdog/chi-080304-magnets-graphic-html,0,1307543.htmlpage.

4. CPSC, "Lead Paint Hazard Found In Four Children's Puzzles," March 4, 1993, http://www.cpsc.gov/cpscpub/prerel/prhtml93/93049.html.

5. CPSC, "Kellogg Company Recalls Bunny Rabbit Because Of Potential Choking Hazards," March 22, 1991, http://www.cpsc.gov/cpscpub/prerel/prhtml91/91056.html.

6. CPSC, "WHAM-O Backyard Water Slides Are Dangerous For Adults And Teenagers," May 27, 1993, http://www.cpsc.gov/cpscpub/prerel/prhtml93/93076.html.

7. CPSC, "CPSC, Toy Manufacturers Announce Recall to Replace Toy Basketball Nets," December 22, 1998, http://www.cpsc.gov/cpscpub/prerel/prhtml99/99036.html.

8. M. Hora and H. Bapuji, "Agility in Reverse Supply Chains: Evidence from Product Recalls in the Toy Industry," paper presented at the Production and Operations Management Society Annual Conference, 2009.

9. Ibid.

8 More Recalls and Even More Harm

1. CPSC, "Bookspan Recalls Discovery Bunny Books Due to Choking Hazard," May 17, 2007, http://www.cpsc.gov/CPSCPUB/PREREL/prhtml07/07551.html.

2. Chen and colleagues use the label *proactive* to denote recalls without incidents, injuries, or deaths, and use the label *passive* to denote those with incidents, injuries, or deaths. Please see Y. Chen, S. Ganesan, and Y. Liu, "Does a Firm's Product-Recall Strategy Affect its Financial Value? An Examination of Strategic Alternatives During Product-Harm Crises," *Journal of Marketing* 73 (2009): 214–226.

We prefer the term *preventive* because the label *proactive* means several things at once, such as swift action or voluntary action. However, not all recalls without incidents are swift, and neither are they always voluntary in that the potential danger may have been noticed by the CPSC in its investigations of toys. Please see M. Hora, H. Bapuji, and A. Roth, "Safety Hazard and Time to Recall: The Role of Recall Strategy, Product Defect type, and Supply Chain Player in the U.S. Toy Industry," working paper, available from the authors.

3. CPSC, "Old Navy Recalls Stuffed Toys; Button Eyes Can Detach and Pose a Choking Hazard to Young Children," February 19, 2009, http://www.cpsc.gov/CPSCPUB/PREREL/prhtml09/09134. html.

4. CPSC, "Child's Death Prompts Replacement Program of Magnetic Building Sets," March 31, 2006, http://www.cpsc.gov/cpscpub/ prerel/prhtml06/06127.html.

5. To ensure robustness of the analysis, an alternative coding was also used in which only the recalls after injuries and deaths occurred were coded as reactive while the recalls without incidents, injuries or deaths were coded as preventive. In other words, the alternative coding omitted the incidents data because incidents may not always demonstrate potential danger. However, the patterns were same using both the coding schemes.

6. J. Garnaut, "Toy-Makers Play the Blame Game," *Sydney Morning Herald*, September 17, 2007, http://www.smh.com.au/news/business/ toymakers-play-the-blame-game/2007/09/16/1189881341230.html.

7. CPSC, "Playskool Voluntarily Recalls Toy Tool Benches after the Death of Two Toddlers," September 22, 2006, http://www.cpsc. gov/cpscpub/prerel/prhtml06/06266.html.

8. CPSC, "Graco Recalls Cradle Portion Of Swing Based On Reports Of Suffocation Incidents," February 24, 1992, http://www.cpsc. gov/CPSCPUB/PREREL/prhtml92/92054.html.

9. For further details, please see E. M. Felcher, *It's No Accident: How Corporations Sell Dangerous Baby Products* (Monroe: Common Courage Press, 2001).

10. CPSC, "Child's Death Prompts Replacement Program of Magnetic Building Sets," March 31, 2006, http://www.cpsc.gov/cpscpub/ prerel/prhtml06/06127.html.

11. CPSC, "Magnetix Magnetic Building Set Recall Expanded," April 19, 2007, http://www.cpsc.gov/CPSCPUB/PREREL/ PRHTML07/07164.html. Around the time of the recall, Rose Art was acquired by Mega Brands. It was later reported that Mega Brands was not made aware of the extent of damage due to magnets issue by Rose Art.

12. CPSC, "Implementation of a Searchable Consumer Product Safety Incident Database," September 10, 2009, http://www.cpsc.gov/ cpscpub/pubs/reports/cpsia212.pdf.

13. CPSC, "Unregulated Products," http://www.cpsc.gov/businfo/ unreg.html.

14. CPSC, *Regulated Products Handbook*, January, 2005, http://www. cpsc.gov/BUSINFO/8001.pdf; "Statement of The Honorable Thomas H. Moore, The Honorable Robert S. Adler, and The Honorable Inez M. Tenenbaum on the Final Interpretive Rule on Civil Penalty Factors," March 10, 2010, http://www.cpsc.gov/pr/ civpen03102010.pdf.

15. CPSC, "CPSC Approves Final Rule on Civil Penalty Factors," March 16, 2010, http://www.cpsc.gov/cpscpub/prerel/prhtml10/10168.html.

16. CPSC, "Brinkmann Corporation to Pay $175,000 to Settle Civil Penalty Case," November 20, 2996, http://www.cpsc.gov/cpscpub/prerel/prhtml97/97025.html.

17. CPSC, "L.L. Bean, Inc. to Pay $750,000 Civil Penalty for Delay in Reporting Backpack Child Carriers," August 30, 2000, http://www.cpsc.gov/cpscpub/prerel/prhtml00/00174.html.

18. Some releases of the CPSC contain multiple companies. For example, release #09–188 of CPSC states that 14 firms have agreed to pay more than $1 million in civil penalties. This notice clubs 14 different cases of violations in one notice. Counting this as one instance would not provide a true picture of the extent of violation. Therefore, for the purposes of this analysis, each case of a fine on each company was coded as a unique instance.

19. CPSC, "CPSC Approves Final Rule on Civil Penalty Factors," March 16, 2010, http://www.cpsc.gov/cpscpub/prerel/prhtml10/10168.html.

20. CPSC, "Kansas Firms to Pay $600,000 Civil Penalty for Selling Banned Fireworks," December 8, 2005, www.cpsc.gov/cpscpub/prerel/prhtml06/06050.html.

21. CPSC, "Great Lakes Products, Inc. Pays To Settle Civil Penalty Case," "September 22, 1994, www.cpsc.gov/cpscpub/prerel/prhtml94/94136.html.

22. CPSC, "Walgreen Co. To Pay $50,000 To Settle Civil Penalty Case," February 28, 1994, www.cpsc.gov/cpscpub/prerel/prhtml94/94040.html.

23. CPSC, "CPSC Settles Flammability Violations With Cotton Cloud Futon," August 22, 1995, www.cpsc.gov/cpscpub/prerel/prhtml95/95158.html.

24. CPSC, "Parent Company of Bloomingdale's/Macy's Pays Record Fine for Selling Flammable Children's Sleepwear," April 12, 2001, www.cpsc.gov/cpscpub/prerel/prhtml01/01123.html.

25. CPSC, "Commission Levies $1.5 Million In Penalties," September 23, 2003, http://www.cpsc.gov/cpscpub/prerel/prhtml03/03188.html.

26. CPSC, "Tennessee Man Sentenced to Prison for Making False Statements to CPSC in Cigarette Lighter Case," April 21, 2000, http://www.cpsc.gov/cpscpub/prerel/prhtml00/00101.html.

9 Increasing Recalls, Decreasing Remedies

1. Sambrook Research International, *Product Recall Research*, commissioned by the Department of Trade and Industry Consumer Affairs Directorate, London, 2000.

At times, recalls are re-announced because of low return rates. For example, Coby electronics announced two recalls of rechargeable batteries sold with portable DVD players (on October 8, 2008 and on October 22, 2009). However, following low return rates and additional reports of fires, the company re-issued the recall six months after its second recall, that is, on April 26, 2010. See CPSC, "Low Return Rate and Additional Reports of Fires Prompt Re-announcement of Coby Electronics Portable DVD/CD/MP3 Player Recalls," April 26, 2010, http://www.cpsc.gov/cpscpub/prerel/prhtml10/10205.html.

2. Ibid. The threshold of low-price in this study, conducted in United Kingdom, was £10.

3. CPSC, "Hasbro, Inc. Recalls to Repair Nerf Blasters; Child's Skin Can Get Caught in Plunger of the Toy," October 9, 2008, http://www.cpsc.gov/cpscpub/prerel/prhtml09/09007.html.

4. CPSC, "Fisher Price Recalls Go Diego Go Boat Toys Due to Violation of Lead Paint Standard,: October 25., 2007, http://www.cpsc.gov/cpscpub/prerel/prhtml08/08048.html; CPSC, "CPSC, Brand Imports, LLC Announce Recall of Children's Rings," March 2, 2004, http://www.cpsc.gov/cpscpub/prerel/prhtml04/04090.html.

5. CPSC, "Dunkin' Donuts Recalls Glow Sticks Due to Choking and Strangulation Hazards," October 17, 2007, www.cpsc.gov/cpscpub/prerel/prhtml08/08030.html.

6. CPSC, "CPSC, IKEA Announce Recall of Stuffed Teddy Bears," October 17, 2002, www.cpsc.gov/cpscpub/prerel/prhtml03/03020.html.

7. CPSC, "Quaker Halts Sales Of Cap'n Crunch Cereal Containing 'Popper' Promotional Toy Because Of Eye Injuries," April 2, 1993, http://www.cpsc.gov/cpscpub/prerel/prhtml93/93065.html.

8. CPSC, "CPSC Announces Recall of Metal Toy Jewelry Sold in Vending Machines," July 8, 2004, http://www.cpsc.gov/cpscpub/prerel/prhtml04/04174.html and CPSC, "CPSC, Brand Imports, LLC Announce Recall of Children's Rings," March 2, 2004, http://www.cpsc.gov/cpscpub/prerel/prhtml04/04090.html.

9. CPSC, "State Farm® Recalls Good Neigh Bears® Due to Choking Hazard," March 17, 2009, http://www.cpsc.gov/cpscpub/prerel/prhtml09/09156.html.

10 Managing Recalls: Before and After

1. L. Tischler, "All About Yves," *Mansueto Ventures*, October 1, 2007, www.fastcompany.com/magazine/119/all-about-yves.html.

2. "Winners Over The Past Five Years," *Business Week*, July 30, 2007, http://www.businessweek.com/magazine/content/07_31/b4044403.htm.

3. H. Beyer and K. Holtzblatt, *Contextual design: Defining Customer-Ccentered Systems* (San Francisco: Morgan Kaufmann, 1998).

4. CPSC, "LeapFrog Recalls to Repair Children's Activity Centers Due to Arm Entrapment Hazard," September 7, 2006, http://www.cpsc.gov/cpscpub/prerel/prhtml06/06253.html.

5. CPSC, "Regent Sports Recalls Soccer Goal Nets Following Strangulation Death of a Child," September 16, 2008, http://www.cpsc.gov/cpscpub/prerel/prhtml08/08400.html.

6. Bapuji H, Beamish P. 2008. Product Recalls: Avoid hazardous design flaws. Harvard Business Review. March:23–26.

7. Felcher M. 2001. *It's No Accident: How Corporations Sell Dangerous Baby Products.* Common Courage Press: Monroe, ME.

8. CPSC, "The Land of Nod Recalls to Repair Cottage Bunk Beds Due to Fall Hazard," February 5, 2009, http://www.cpsc.gov/cpscpub/prerel/prhtml09/09720.html.

9. CPSC, "Fisher-Price Recalls Learning Pots and Pans™ Toys Due to Choking Hazard," August 7, 2008, http://www.cpsc.gov/cpscpub/prerel/prhtml08/08362.html.

10. Based on conversations with importers.

11. Character Group plc, "Bindeez Hints and Tips," http://www.character-online.com/bindeez-QA/.

12. CPSC, "Pressure Cookers Recalled By Manttra Inc. Due to Burn Hazard," December 21, 2007, http://www.cpsc.gov/cpscpub/prerel/prhtml08/08147.html.

13. CPSC, "Playskool Voluntarily Recalls Toy Tool Benches after the Death of Two Toddlers," September 22, 2006, http://www.cpsc.gov/cpscpub/prerel/prhtml06/06266.html.

14. M. Hora and H. Bapuji, "Agility in Reverse Supply Chains: Evidence from Product Recalls in the Toy Industry," paper presented at the Production and Operations Management Society Annual Conference, 2009.

15. CPSC, "Sears Warns Consumers to Remove Label from Craftsman Circular Saws, Obstructed Blade Guard Poses Laceration Hazard," April 5, 2007, http://www.cpsc.gov/cpscpub/prerel/prhtml07/07149.html.

16. CPSC, "CPSC, Toys"R"Us Announce Recall of Children's Soap Craft Set," December 24, 1997, http://www.cpsc.gov/cpscpub/prerel/PRHTML98/98049.html.

17. H. Bapuji and M. Crossan, "Knowledge Types and Knowledge Management Strategies" in M. Gibbert and T. Durand (eds), *Strategic Networks: Learning To Compete.* Blackwell: Malden, MA.

18. S. Lee, N. Beck , and H. Kim, "Mischievous Magnets: Unexpected Health Hazard in Children," *Journal of Pediatric Surgery* 31, no. 12 (1996): 1694–1695.

19. T. J. Garfinkle, "A Most Attractive Nose," *New England Journal of Medicine* 338 (1998): 1474.

20. S. McCormick, P. Brennan, J. Yassa, and R. Shawis, "Children and Mini-Magnets: An Almost Fatal Attraction," *Emergency Medicine Journal* 19 (2001): 71–73.

11 Managing Recalls: Everybody's Business

1. Beamish P, Bapuji H. 2008. "Toy Recalls and China: Emotion vs. Evidence." Management and Organization Review 4, no. 2:197–209.
2. For further details on recalls research, please see M. Etayankara and H. Bapuji, "Product Recalls: A Review of Literature," *Proceedings of Annual Meeting of Administrative Sciences Association of Canada*, Niagara Falls, Canada, 2009. The literature review presented in this paper formed the basis for providing several directions for future research.
3. G. Jarrell and S. Peltzman, "The Impact of Product Recalls on the Wealth of Sellers," *Journal of Political Economy* 93 (1985): 512–536. A. A. Marcus, P. Bromiley, and R. Goodman, "Preventing Corporate Crises: Stock Market Losses as a Deterrent to the Production of Hazardous Products," *Columbia Journal of World Business* 22, no. 1 (1987): 33.

   D. Dranove and C. Olsen, "The Economic Side Effects of Dangerous Drug Announcements," *Journal of Law and Economics.* 37 (1994): 323–348.

   B. M. Barber and M. N. Darrough, "Product Reliability & Firm value. The Experience of American & Japanese Automakers, 1972–1992," *Journal of Political Economy* 104 no. 5 (1996).
4. G. E. Hoffer, S. W. Pruitt, and R. J. Reilly, "The Impact of Product Recalls on the Wealth of Sellers: A Re-Examination," *Journal of Political Economy* 96: 663–670.
5. E. T. Cheah, W. L. Chan, and C. Chieng, "The Corporate Social Responsibility of Pharmaceutical Product Recalls: An Empirical Examination of US and UK Markets," *Journal of Business Ethics* 76, no. 4 (2007): 427–449.

   T. H. Chu, C. C. Lin, and L. J. Prather, "An Extension of Security Price Reactions Around Product Recall Announcements," *Quarterly Journal of Business and Economics* 44 (Fall 2005): 33–49.

   S. W. Pruitt and D. R. Peterson, "Security Price Reactions Around Product Recall Announcements," *Journal of Financial Research* 9, no. 2 (1986): 113–122.

   M. R. Thomsen and A. M. McKenzie, "Market Incentives for Safe Foods: An Examination of Shareholder Losses from Meat and Poultry Recalls," *American Journal of Agricultural Economics* 83, no. 3 (2001): 526–538.
6. M. R. Thomsen, R. Shiptsova, and S. J. Hamm, "Sales Responses to Recalls for Listeria Monocytogenes: Evidence from Branded Ready-to-Eat Meats," *Review of Agricultural Economics* 28, no. 4 (2006): 482–493.

R. J. Reilly and G.E. Hoffer, "Will Retarding the Information Flow on Automobile Recalls Affect Consumer Demand?" *Economic Inquiry* 21, no. 3 (1983): 444–447.

C. F. Keown, "Consumer Reactions to Food and Drug Product Recalls: A Case Study of Hawaiian Consumers," *Journal of Consumer Policy* 11, no. 2 (1988): 209.

7. P. Bromiley and A. Marcus, "The Deterrent to Dubious Corporate Behaviour: Profitability, Probability and Safety Recalls," *Strategic Management Journal* 10 (1989): 233–250.

8. J. Klein and N. Dawar, "Corporate Social Responsibility and Consumers' Attributions and Brand Evaluations in a Product-Harm Crisis," *International Journal of Research in Marketing* 21, no. 3 (2004): 203–217; J.C. Mowen, "Further Information on Consumer Perceptions on Product Recalls," *Advances in Consumer Research* 7, no. 1 (1980): 519–523; F. Dardis and M. M. Haigh, "Prescribing Versus Describing: Testing Image Restoration Strategies in a Crisis Situation," *Corporate Communications* 14, no. 1 (): 101–118; N. Dawar, "Product Harm Crisis and Signaling Ability of Brands," *International Studies of Management & Organization* 28, no. 3 (1998): 109–119.

9. Reuters, "Topps Meat Goes Out of Business After Recall," October 6, 2007, http://www.reuters.com/article/idUSWNAS5-66620071006.

10. P. R. Haunschild and M. Rhee, "The Role of Volition in Organizational Learning: The Case of Automotive Product Recalls," *Management Science* 50, no. 11 (2004): 1545–1560.

11. "Two-thirds of Total Number: Design Flaws Blamed in Auto Recalls," *The Victoria Advocate,* December 16, 1976, 9D.

12. G. Rider, "CPSC Testing Rule Should Include Design Analysis," *Product Safety Letter,* April 16, 2010, http://www.productsafetyletter.com/news/6396-1.html.

13. Beamish P, Bapuji H. "Toy Recalls and China."

14. Carvalho S, Muralidharan E, Bapuji H. 2010. *Consumers' Attribution of Blame in Product-Harm Crises Involving Hybrid Products.* German-French-Austrian Conference on Marketing: Vienna, Austria.

Epilogue   Accelerating Cars, Contaminated Medicines, and Continuing Recalls

1. K. M. McDonald, *Shifting Out of Park: Moving Auto Safety from Recalls to Reason* (Tucson, AZ: Lawyers and Judges Publishing Company, 2006).

2. National Public Radio, "Unintended Acceleration Not Limited To Toyotas," March 3, 2010, http://www.npr.org/templates/story/story.php?storyId=124276771&ps=rs and National Public Radio Vehicle Acceleration Complaints Database, Available from: http://www.npr.org/templates/story/story.php?storyId=124235858.

3. H. Tabuchi, "Little Help in Japan for Owners of Toyotas With Acceleration Problems," *New York Times,* March 5, 2010, http://www.nytimes.com/2010/03/06/business/global/06toyota.html?hpw.

4. BBC World News, "Toyota Pressed by US Watchdog over Recall Speed," February 17, 2010, http://news.bbc.co.uk/2/hi/business/8519306.stm.

5. H. Jenkins, "My Sudden Acceleration Nightmare," *Wall Street Journal,* February 24, 2010, http://online.wsj.com/article/SB10001424052748704506104575083180509210638.html.

6. Mira Oberman, "Is US bullying Toyota on recall?" *Associated Press,* February 3, 2010, http://www.google.com/hostednews/afp/article/ALeqM5im7AzPBsRb2Q_qT0FXa8DxrjjLwA.

7. P. Shrivastava, I. I. Mitroff, D. Miller, and A. Miglani, "Understanding Industrial Crises," *The Journal of Management Studies,* 25, no. 4 (1988): 285–303 and G. J. Siomkos, "On Achieving Exoneration After a Product Safety Industrial Crisis," *The Journal of Business and Industrial Marketing,* 14, no. 1(1999): 17–29.

8. P. Kavilanz, "Tylenol Maker Scrambles to Fix Quality Problem," *CNN Money,* May 6, 2010, http://money.cnn.com/2010/05/03/news/companies/Tylenol_maker_McNeil_recalls_persist and
P. Kavilanz, "Bacteria Identified in Tylenol Recall," *CNN Money,* May 6, 2010, http://money.cnn.com/2010/05/05/news/companies/childrens_tylenol_recall_bacteria.

9. H. Bapuji, "Maytag Needs to Ponder Slow Recalls," *Winnipeg Free Press.* May 4, 2009, http://www.winnipegfreepress.com/local/Maytag-needs-to-ponder-slow-recalls-44315052.html.

10. H. Bapuji, "McDonald's Shrek Recall: More Questions than Answers," *Strategy and You,* June 2010, http://www.strategyandyou.org/2010/06/mcdonald-shrek-recall-more-questions.html.

Index